Merry Christmas, Dad,
love,
Bob and Maureen

The Armbro Story

The Armbro Story

Peter Lewington

Burns & MacEachern Limited

Toronto

Grateful acknowledgement is made to the Ontario Ministry of Natural Resources for their kind
permission to reproduce the portion of their map in the illustrations.

The publisher wishes to express sincere appreciation to Wray Featherston
for his assistance in the design and production of this book.

Editing
Laura Damania, Scarborough, Ontario

Dust Jacket Design
N. Milton, Design Work Shop, Toronto, Ontario

Typesetting and Printing
Ronalds Federated Graphics, Richmond Hill, Ontario

Binding
The Hunter Rose Company, Don Mills, Ontario

Library of Congress Catalog Card Number 74-84382

ISBN 0-88768-053-4

Printed and bound in Canada

Elgin and Victoria Armstrong greet Her Majesty Queen Elizabeth the Queen Mother during her 1962 visit to Canada.

Contents

FOREWORD

I have not known Elgin Armstrong personally very long, but I have heard of his farming, construction and horses for thirty years.

In the early 1940s he was known in the south Huron area of Ontario, near Exeter where I made my home in 1944, as the contractor who built runways at the Royal Canadian Air Force Flying Training School at Centralia; he had done the same at Sky Harbour and Port Albert near Goderich.

The business I operated in Exeter, and subsequently in London and Crediton, was involved in the accumulation, processing and distribution of good seed. Elgin Armstrong had earlier achieved a reputation for quality as a grower and custom thresher of clover and alfalfa in Peel County which was famous, among other things, for the production of alfalfa seed. He was one of the first farmers to grow alfalfa and was a prize winner for his seed at the first Royal Agricultural Winter Fair.

Shortly after my appointment as Minister of Highways for Ontario in 1962, I met Elgin. I had previously heard about him from my staff who described him as a "good, reliable road builder," adding that he was tough but fair to deal with and "a stickler for quality and propriety." That was, as time and events proved, a fair, honest description of a fair, capable and honest man.

I recall that in 1967 Armstrong Brothers Company Limited was awarded a construction contract for ten miles of King Highway Number 4 from the north limits of Exeter. The work was accomplished in the usual "Armbro style." Excellent detours were provided. The work was tidily done and the adjoining farmers were fairly dealt with. At night, the equipment—trucks, bulldozers, graders, compacters, et cetera—were taken to one farm, where space was rented, and stored until the next day. Farm entrances were all restored and, to my knowledge, if farm drains were interfered with at all, they were all replaced to the farmers' complete satisfaction.

The result is ten miles of fine highway, as good today as it was on completion, and no unhappy constituents. Armbro style all the way.

Another incident which interested me mightily illustrates Elgin's desire to be in the forefront in keeping abreast of the times; this characteristic has been marked from his earliest days, when material was excavated and moved with horses and men driving wagons and using scoops or hand-operated, horse-drawn graders. Now, strong backs and shovels have been replaced by monstrous power equipment.

In 1971 the Armstrongs purchased a slip-form concrete paver which could lay concrete to a depth of fifteen inches and a width of twenty-five feet without any forms. This type of construction had never been approved by the Canada Department of Transport. However, the DOT allowed a test of the paver for the building of Toronto's International Airport. The results met specifications and the Armstrongs were allowed to use it as long as results were as good as the test section.

Recently, the slip-form construction was used at Montreal's Mirabel Airport at Ste Scholastique. These two large airport contracts have been completed using new, modern equipment because Elgin Armstrong had vision and confidence. Vision and confidence from which the people of Canada are the beneficiaries.

The name "Armbro," an abbreviation of Armstrong Brothers, is the current corporate style. But in some areas the brothers Elgin and Ted Armstrong are best known for the ABC prefix; this originally stood for their Armstrong Brothers Construction partnership and latterly for the incorporated Armstrong Brothers Company. ABC Farms Limited is known around the world for the breeding of Holstein-Friesian dairy cattle and

X

standardbred racing horses; being satisfied with nothing but the best in quality and performance has brought justly earned recognition, fame and respect to Elgin Armstrong.

Raising the greatest Holstein bull in the world has to be the ultimate satisfaction a breeder can enjoy; this came to Elgin with ABC Reflection Sovereign out of ABC Inka May, a top producing cow. ABC bloodlines have won championships throughout North America and sell for record prices throughout the world.

I saw Elgin from yet another vantage point in the late 1960s when I was Treasurer of Ontario; the Ontario Racing Commission was one of a number of government commissions and agencies reporting through the treasurer of the province to the Legislature.

It was an opportunity to learn about horse racing and it prepared me for my present position as chairman of the Ontario Racing Commission. I got to know many of the people who helped make horse racing a leading industry and a great sport; I shortly learned that among the many dedicated men, particularly on the standardbred side, was Elgin Armstrong.

The Armbro standardbreds are recognized in North America and abroad because Elgin acquired Adios mares and bred them to the fastest stallions in America. He set out to win every major standardbred stakes in America. The record shows that he succeeded. His present ambition is to have an Armbro-bred horse win every major stakes race.

When one looks back over the years, starting when Elgin took on the responsibility of the family farm in Peel County at the age of fourteen, and observes his unswerving insistence on quality and performance, there can be no doubt that his goal has been achieved, and any more he desires to set for himself will also be attained.

Toronto. July, 1974.   CHARLES S. MACNAUGHTON

PREFACE

"**I**'D like to meet Elgin Armstrong and go to the standardbred races" were the first reactions of my publisher, Barney Sandwell, president of Burns & MacEachern, on reading *The Armbro Story*. I hope that other readers will feel the same.

There would have been no Armbro story without Elgin's flair for building things and inspiring people. His anecdotes and dry humour added to my enjoyment in researching and writing this story of Canadian achievement. My sincere thanks go to Dr. Glen Brown for his unfailing courtesy and inexhaustible fund of information on every facet of the trotters and pacers.

I am grateful to the Armstrong family and Armbro executives for their responses during extensive interviews; their frankness is especially valued, as it was clearly understood from the outset that neither the family nor the Armbro executives would see the book before publication.

To Jack McArthur I owe a debt of gratitude for his card-index memory for everything from cows and companies to horses and highway construction. He has that rare ability to be close to people and events and still remain objective. His pertinent comments and criticisms have contributed to whatever virtues this book may possess; any shortcomings are my own.

And just how do I acknowledge the contributions of my wife Jean? She calved our cows in my absence and typed the transcripts of innumerable taped interviews upon my return. She also typed the entire manuscript, and should any passage lack clarity it is probably because I have failed to take her wise counsel.

Larigmoor Farm,   PETER LEWINGTON
Ilderton, Ontario,
Canada. July, 1974.

The Armbro Story

Chapter 1

ELGIN

"ELGIN Armstrong has a gift which the rest of us missed. He could look at a horse and tell you how fast it could run. He could look at a cow and tell you how much milk she should give. He could look at a man and tell you how much work he could do; there are few like him on earth," says George Cowan, an avid Elgin watcher ever since he began working for the Armstrong Brothers Company in 1934.

Cowan's appraisal is typical of an atypical situation. Cowan has seen Elgin under every conceivable circumstance, from the Great Depression and World War II to the booms and recessions of the postwar years. It is said that no man is a hero to his valet; but Elgin has forged lasting bonds of affection with everyone who has been involved in a shoestring operation which grew to employ some two thousand men and gross some seventy million dollars annually.

George Cowan is a director of the Armbro family of companies; his special responsibility has been paving. That's everything from the road to the gates of Banff National Park, to Highway 401, and the runways at Toronto's International Airport to Montreal's new Mirabel Airport at Ste Scholastique. At nineteen, he was a deckhand on a scow, building Lake Erie breakwaters. He came to the struggling construction company of brothers Elgin and Ted Armstrong as a foreman. He moved steadily up the ladder. As the Armstrong enterprises prospered, some things never

3

changed. Elgin remained the shrewd, tough operator with a leavening sense of humour and a gift for motivating people. The rapport with his earliest workers never changed either. Cowan says, "In some companies you'd have to make an appointment to see the president. But with the Armstrongs, if you have a problem, you just march in and tell them to go to hell!"

Norman Smith, the president of International Harvester Company of Canada, heads a business which differs in every aspect of its corporate structure from the Armstrongs'. Despite the many differences, the liaison between the two companies has been steadily maturing for some forty-five years. Norman Smith sees Elgin as "a real gentleman. He is a completely considerate fellow, shrewd, honest and never afraid to take a chance. He likes fair play. Perhaps his most notable characteristic is his foresight. He has had steadfast faith in the tremendous growth potential in Ontario and Canada."

Conn Smythe, the entrepreneur who built among other things Maple Leaf Gardens, sees Elgin as "a great Canadian." Conn Smythe and Elgin Armstrong belong to that breed of self-starters who, for better or for worse, have left their indelible stamp on Canada. They share the same small-c conservative outlook, a faith in such institutions as the monarchy and the Commonwealth and such old-fashioned virtues as integrity. When Conn Smythe and Elgin Armstrong reach agreement there's a shake of the hand; not for them, a battery of high-priced lawyers.

"The Armstrongs are the best road contractors in Canada," declares Conn Smythe. "I've known of Elgin for nearly fifty years and have done business with him in many ways. I've sat on the board of the Ontario Jockey Club with him. A lot of people hear a statement from such big shots as E. P. Taylor and wonder if they shouldn't march in line with him. But Elgin has his own ideas and he doesn't scare for anybody."

Clarence Charters, a bright and active octogenarian, sees Elgin from the vantage of the Peel County Establishment. Clarence Charters' father Samuel was publisher of *The Conservator* which he purchased in 1890. The very title of the paper was in keeping with the times in which a paper was either Whig or Tory and there was no middle ground. However, a prominent quotation in an old copy of *The Conservator* adheres to the belief that "A good press is as essential to a country's well-being as a good govern-

4

ment and the one is often the best security for the other." Samuel Charters took his politics beyond the editorial page: he served in both the Ontario Legislature and the House of Commons; as a member of parliament, he was chief whip under two prime ministers, R. B. Bennett and Arthur Meighen, who were to share equally unhappy political fates.

Clarence Charters inherited the publisher's chair of *The Conservator*. In his own right, he went on to become national organizer of the Conservative party in Canada and for many years was managing director of the Canadian Weekly Newspaper Association. His avid interest in sports has not been dimmed by his eighty-two years. Back in the 1930s, he was a member of the Canadian Lacrosse Championship team, along with the father of Ontario's present premier, Bill Davis. Lacrosse is really Canada's national game and has continued its close association with Brampton. A subsequent member of the Lacrosse Hall of Fame, George Thompson, in the 1950s and 1960s coached Armstrong-sponsored teams to the Ontario championships. On another three occasions, Brampton teams went all the way to become Canadian Junior Champions.

Clarence Charters says, "Elgin Armstrong is a gambler. But he also had an intuitive sense which enabled him to appraise a situation. Then he would act decisively." Mr. Charters has an added incentive for watching the progress of the Armstrong brothers; his son, Bob, is president of the Armbro group of companies.

Doug Middlebrook is, like Elgin, a former Peel County farm boy; he once farmed beside the Armstrongs in Derry West. Middlebrook, who subsequently worked for Armstrong Brothers for many years, latterly as a superintendent, turned out on a cold winter's night to give his recollections of Elgin. "The old man is one hell of a fine guy and we'd do anything for him."

Bill Willis was later to own a heavy construction equipment company in Toronto; he first came into the Armstrongs' orbit when he was installed as office manager of ABC by Elgin's creditors during a critical time of the depression. "Elgin?" asked Willis. "He's a long-headed old bugger. When a quarry he was working at Trois Pistoles in Quebec ran out, he managed to unload the equipment to a competitor, once the word got around that he was moving to Montreal to set up in opposition! Even a pile

5

of stone which was left over and thought to be of little value, he sold for $100,000. Elgin has a tremendous memory and can recall details of trans-actions or quotations months later. I remember I called him about a power shovel which I quoted at $63,000. His response was, 'But you quoted me $61,500 four months ago'; so he got the shovel at the earlier quotation. But it was not needed, as the contract for which it was ordered fell through. Un-deterred, Elgin invited me to watch the thoroughbreds at the old Woodbine track. Between races, he sold the unwanted shovel at a profit to another contractor he spied in the stand."

Dr. Glen Brown, manager of ABC Farms, has risen to prominence in international standardbred circles with the success of the Armbro horses. Brown recalls, "We were getting ready to go to the races and sales at Lexington, Kentucky, when in came Elgin's accountant and laid down the law. 'Things are kind of tight and on no account are you to buy anything!' he told Elgin, meanwhile hammering the desk to emphasize his point. I drove Elgin for perhaps twenty minutes in an unaccustomed silence as we headed for Lexington. Then he got his cigar going and asked me, 'What do you like in the catalogue, Glen?' I responded with some surprise, and told him I thought we weren't going to buy anything. But of course we did."

By now, Glen Brown has become accustomed to Elgin's mercurial moods at a sale. "I remember we once went to a Holstein-Friesian sale at Trafalgar, where the auctioneer was Harry Hays who later became Canada's minister of agriculture and a senator. I thought that we had at-tended the sale in a mood of nostalgia to see some of the descendants of the long since dispersed ABC Holstein herd put up for sale. He precipitately bought two bulls, although he was never again to own a cow! The bulls were grandsons of ABC Reflection Sovereign and, according to Elgin, 'We can't let that blood leave the country!' "

Forty thousand dollars is a goodly chunk of money to invest in an un-proven bull. But, like so many Elgin hunches, this one also paid off. When Elgin purchased the Holstein-Friesian bull Agro Acres Never Fear he knew that he was buying the blood of cattle he had himself bred in earlier years. What he couldn't know, but obviously suspected, was the bull's ability to transmit desirable qualities to his offspring. The worth of a bull is measured in two ways. He is personally rated for his own physique and conformation. In that department, Agro Acres Never Fear is given the accolade of Excellent. The other yardstick is the prepotency of a bull to transmit the good qualities which are already known to exist in his pedigree. Never Fear is aptly named. His first 111 classified daughters are well above the breed average for conformation, or type. Some of those daughters have gone on to be show winners.

George Cowan's appraisal of Elgin is not far from the mark. The ABC Holstein-Friesians rank with such herds as Montvic and Rosafe as the jewels in the Canadian dairy breed's crown.

The Armstrong standardbred horses have won almost every major race in the world at least once: Helicopter at the Hambletonian; Dottie's Pick at the American Classic; Countess Adios at the Messenger Stakes; Armbro Flight at the Roosevelt International; and Sunnie Tar who raced more two-minute miles than any other mare. Such sires as Armbro Duke, Governor Armbro, Eagle Armbro and Armbro Hurricane are at stud in various parts of the world where they are upgrading the sport.

Two out of three: Cowan is dead-on with his appraisal of Elgin and his eye for fast horses and productive dairy cattle. But how about the most important ingredient in any business, people? Old employees, like Allan Barr, have recently retired, having never worked for anyone but Elgin. A former truck driver heads the multi-million-dollar Construction Equipment Division, a former raker of asphalt is senior vice-president and the erstwhile water boy is president. Looking back over such a varied business and sporting career, Elgin's own chief pleasure is in "having picked so many good men and having them all come through with flying colours."

Elgin was equally fortunate in the women in his life. He married his childhood sweetheart, Victoria Lawrence, who was to bear him five children and share his love for horses. Victoria Armstrong did not live in the shadow of her forceful husband. The tack room at the ABC Farms at Brampton has a suite with prize-winning rosettes covering the walls like confetti. Victoria Armstrong was a consistent winner with her hackney ponies in such major shows as Chicago, New York and Louisville and she was also a familiar sight at Ontario's country fairs.

I first met Elgin in the spring of 1971, when I began digging into the Armbro story. He was seventy-four and looked it. Construction is a rugged business for younger men, yet Elgin was only just relinquishing the reins. While he had never known a day's sickness in his working life, he was then slowed down by diabetes. He had had double cataract operations and needed dark glasses to relieve his eyes from the painful glare of the light. At the same time, Victoria was critically ill with cancer. Elgin was not at his best and I got only flashes indicating the man he had once been . . . and would be again. Instead of strolling over from the construction office to the horse barns, Elgin, Jack McArthur, former banker and now an Armbro director, and myself climbed into the air-conditioned Cadillac. I wondered what I was getting into, in a larger sense, as we rode in opulence through the horse barns where the inhabitants' every need is pandered to.

But Elgin is nothing if not resilient. Most people don't live to be two hundred years of age but he gives the impression that if anyone is going to break the rules it will be Elgin.

The surrendering of responsibility to his son Charlie and other executives placed other strains on this self-willed, self-reliant man whose style was to go it alone. Subsequently, when he lost his mate of nearly fifty years, the standardbred horses became an outlet for his restless energy. He mastered, with some difficulty, contact lenses and gradually began to view the world with renewed interest.

A loner in business, in private life he needed company. He found it in the person of Vivian Kuth, widow of the legal counsel for the United States Trotting Association.

"One spring evening I sat with Mr. Armstrong on the lawn of his Lauderdale-by-the-Sea home bordering the Inter-coastal Waterway," recalls Vivian. "This was the first time I had ever been alone with him. He suddenly said, 'Have you ever thought of getting married again, Mrs. Kuth?' I replied that I had not given it much thought and he shot back, 'Would you marry me?' "

"Well, Mr. Armstrong, I'd have to give that some thought," answered Vivian Kuth. If Elgin can be forceful and direct, he had found his match in Mrs. Kuth. After fully two minutes' deliberation she replied, "Yes. I'll marry you—but don't you think, Mr. Armstrong, that if we are going to get married we should know each other by our first names? Mine's Vivian."

Elgin concluded the brief, phlegmatic courtship with a brisk, "It's a

8

deal then. Shake on it!" And he thrust out his hand to cement the agreement.

Elgin had one more romantic question: "How long are you going to stall?"

That was on April 5, 1973. Nine days later they were married, with Howard and Ann Beissinger as the only witnesses. This was a fast event even for Beissinger, who is known for pacing the mile in 1:56 and two-fifths!

Elgin had wisely consulted his housekeeper, Mrs. Lorraine Bailey, about remarriage: "If you're going to get married, Mr. Armstrong—then she's the one." Those nine days were trying ones for Mrs. Bailey, who had to keep the secret even from her husband Arthur, who had taken over as Elgin's chauffeur. Deciding whom to invite and whom not to invite to a twilight-years wedding is a difficult decision. It reaches back to twelve step-grandchildren and fifteen grandchildren. As time was too short to notify everyone, there was nothing for it but a *fait accompli*.

But it was Elgin who nearly blew his cool. Phil Doucet, a long-time friend of Elgin and Charlie who was also staying at the Florida home, was surprised to find Elgin sitting on his bed at 3 A.M. smoking a cigar. His curiosity was further aroused when he averted a tragedy by discovering that Elgin had placed the lighted cigar in the pocket of his new sports jacket.

"They're just like a couple of kids," says Jack McArthur happily. McArthur was the first banker to have confidence in Elgin. Like just about everybody else who has befriended Elgin, the original business transactions have long since been supplanted by friendship and understanding.

Not that Elgin requires much understanding. He says what he means and means what he says. He is essentially the same forthright farm boy whose first off-farm job was working a scraper behind a team of horses. He has nurtured the Armbro companies to the point where individual pieces of equipment may require the investment of a million dollars and a single road-building contract may exceed ten million dollars.

His successes on the racetracks have brought him directorships of the Ontario Jockey Club, the Hambletonian Society, the Standardbred Breeders Association Incorporated and the Hall of Fame of the Trotter.

But for all that, if Elgin were to draft his own epitaph it would be "The best damn farmer in Peel County."

To Ed Bradley, director of racing for the Ontario Jockey Club, he is always "the Governor." When Ted Armstrong wants to cut his brother down to size, he'll use the nickname "Squirt." A source of amusement to some Armstrong executives is son Charlie's ambivalence. When he agrees with his father, it's "Dad"; when he disagrees, it's "Elgin."

To the construction superintendents who have been consistently achieving the impossible, Elgin Armstrong is the man who has the knack of appearing just as everything is shut down for a coffee break. He is the deflator-supreme and he always has a barbed needle if he suspects any slackness.

This Grade 4 graduate has more flair for management than you'll find in your Ivy League school of business administration. Elgin also knows the value of remembering the names and faces of workers. A man is spurred from enthusiasm to dedication when he finds that the boss can even remember his children's names, gleaned at a gathering perhaps a year before.

Elgin knows too the worth of a joke or a smile and an expression of confidence when the work is hopelessly behind schedule and the equipment is mired in mud.

It's "Boss," "Governor," mostly "Elgin" but never "Mr. Armstrong." John Maudsley, some-time asphalt raker, some-time construction superintendent and now an Armbro vice-president charged with generating future company initiatives, says, "If I get too complacent, Elgin will chop me down to size for some petty indiscretion such as failing to have the grass mown. But he is a very different man when he knows I've had all I can take. As a young construction superintendent, I was eager to earn a reputation for doing the job right and ahead of schedule. On a sewer installation, I must have been in too much of a hurry and used an excessive amount of dynamite. After the charge went off, I saw the verger of a nearby church come panting down the street.

" 'Would you please come up to the church; your blasting has done a little damage,' said the mild-mannered verger.

"When we peered in the church door I was horrified. I was stunned by

10

that 'little bit of damage.' The church pews were as uneven as the waves of an angry sea. I had done at least twenty-thousand-dollars' damage—at a time when a dollar really was worth something. Also, twenty thousand dollars was a significant amount in the company budget at that time. With considerable agitation, I telephoned Elgin."

"Yes, yes, John," Elgin's voice crackled over the telephone line. "Now, tell me, John, how's the weather up there? Oh, that's great. Now do you need anything sent up there, John? Do you need any more equipment?"

What is that special alchemy which makes workers redouble their efforts, not just because the boss is there, but because the boss makes them feel good?

We arrive unexpectedly at the Caledon aggregate plant. We are welcomed by Jim Anderson, the superintendent, with the broadest of grins. Anderson salutes Elgin with, "Hi, Dad! You're looking sharp today!" He reaches across Elgin and helps himself from the package of Marguerite cigars, sitting, inevitably, on the dashboard.

Bill Fleming, senior vice-president with International Harvester, shows that he has been covertly observing Elgin. "He gives the impression of being gruff and abrupt but he has the ability to claim tremendous allegiance from his staff. While he is always in a hurry, he still adheres to the nice courtesies of life which are so often overlooked. He is a strong competitor but in everything he has a great sense of humour. He is one of a kind. We'll not see his like again. When they made Elgin Armstrong, they destroyed the mould."

Chapter 2

THE WINNER'S TOUCH

"**E**LGIN could fall into an outhouse and come out smelling like a rose" is the considered opinion of Armbro job superintendent Bill Wright. Lady Luck does not bestow her bounties equitably. Some people are lucky but the luckiest of all are those who enjoy a reputation for being lucky. It is that strange, indefinable quality which lifts a fortunate few out of the crowd.

Bill Wright knows the value of luck. He is responsible for the Mississauga Valley Development which extends to some three thousand acres. This is typical of some of the larger residential and commercial projects. There's a shopping concourse in the centre and a residential project which may take twenty years to complete. While ground is being broken in one section, the finishing touches are being made to sodded boulevards in other areas.

"We have good planning. There's a weekly planning meeting so that we know ahead of time where everyone will be and what they're responsible for. It's a blend of initiative and autonomy. The total effort is coordinated but, as a job superintendent, I can make flexible decisions. There's no bureaucracy," says Bill Wright. "Planning is fine, but without that reputation for luck it may not be enough."

Gene McKinnon is one of a handful of general superintendents. "There is such a thing as the Armstrong luck," Gene says. "The men on

12

the job feel it. No matter how badly a job is going there's an unspoken confidence that somehow it will all come out right. The men don't drag their feet to keep a job going for fear of being laid off. Crews compete with each other to get a job done ahead of schedule. We have a sense of achievement and are quite sure there will be another job to move on to."

Luck? If you're planning on being born on a family farm and aspire to becoming an entrepreneurial contractor, then Derry West is an ideal place. The Armstrong brothers, Elgin and Ted, were born in an area which subsequently became the centre of the most rapid urban development in Canada. It's a communications centre with Highway 401 and Toronto International Airport on the doorstep. And when a massive new development is to be opened, it is always nice to have the premier of the province around to snip the ribbon; the incumbent and also a recent premier both hail from Peel County.

When Elgin decided to forsake thoroughbred horses for standard-breds, it occured to him that an agreeable way to start would be to win the prestigious Hambletonian. He came across Del Miller who was embarking on his phenomenal success which was heightened by the prepotent sire Adios. (Miller has shown himself to be the complete sportsman, who has benefited standardbred racing in many ways. He is a past-president of the Grand Circuit and, as breeder, trainer or driver, his name keeps cropping up.) There has to be a little bit of luck when you buy a mare like Helicopter who promptly wins the Hambletonian and leaves behind a filly such as Armbro Flight who became a world-beating trotter who won almost one half-million dollars in prizes and is now an Armbro brood mare.

One summer's day Elgin and George Cowan were out checking construction sites in northern Ontario. They paused at a hotel in North Bay and overheard a chance conversation. Apparently a lumber company required a road. Elgin and George went out, as Elgin recalls, to "look the situation over." In a short sortie through the bush they stumbled across a strategically located gravel deposit. By the time they'd walked back to the road, Elgin had figured out a quotation for the job. A telephone call revealed that the lumber company was "high-class." The estimate was revised upward . . . and accepted. Elgin has an instinct for what the traffic will bear.

The year that wheat is a good price, Elgin has a large acreage and a good crop. He's hardly installed in his newly acquired Lauderdale-by-the-Sea residence than the bougainvilleas, poinsettias and hibiscus bloom like no others on the Inter-coastal Waterway. The avocados, the orange and the grapefruit trees all have an abundance of fruit. A green thumb is part of the winner's touch.

Not that everything always works out. Elgin wilfully bought Wells Construction in Edmonton against the vehement protestations of his son Charlie. This proved to be one of the more disastrous ventures and was unloaded as soon as possible. It's no surprise that Elgin is fresh out of anecdotes about Wells!

Sometimes things go sour because people have failed to produce. "Well," rationalizes Elgin on such occasions, "he was just a city man. Very few of those city men ever work out!" Sophisticated, young, urban men from the best schools and universities just don't have "the high calibre of the farm boys." Farm boys like Jimmy Brown who is recognized as a potential leader and is soon promoted to superintend a three-million-dollar construction job. Elgin likes the brighter young men from Ontario farms because they are self-starters, weaned on hard work.

There is a remarkable continuity within the Armstrong companies for opportunities to move up the management ladder. Bob Lowndes was a vice-president at forty and in charge of all construction. Lowndes remembers: "I was hitchhiking one day when I was picked up by the engineer of the Township of Toronto. I was the third employee of the department and began as a rod man assisting the survey. After five years I was in charge of all maintenance but had nowhere to go. Charlie Armstrong wanted someone for some of the smaller paving jobs and I just grew with the company."

Very few Armbro people in senior management have come from other companies. Almost to a man, they associate with Ted or Elgin or Charlie. What they do share is an incredible loyalty to the company.

"They always encourage you to do things and leave you thinking that you can achieve," says George Cowan. "A person thinks, 'My goodness, if he's got that much faith in me, then I should be able to do it.' This just seems to bring out the best in people."

The best or the worst? Alan DeVries is a foreman of a water mains crew. He is a mild-mannered, gentlemanly fellow who belies the reputation the construction industry has for rough, tough workers with a limited, but colourful vocabulary. But one hot summer's day I came across DeVries when his long-suffering patience had been tried to its capacity. Normally, the roads and services are completed before work is begun on house building. But there was DeVries, trying to install a water main while a housing contractor had the gall to dump the dirt from basement excavations right in DeVries' path; not only that, he had pumps gushing water so that they eroded the water main excavation.

"If they want to be cruel, then we have to give them some of the same medicine," said DeVries. "I soon put a stop to that builder's nonsense. I gave him a choice of quitting or having his basements filled in by one of our bulldozers." There just has to be a winner's touch when a foreman in a company, with over two thousand people on the payroll, acts like an aggressive capitalist.

As the unremitting flow of new technology floods an already sophisticated world, so procedures and computerized systems tend to supplant the individual. There was a machine at Expo '67, the world fair and frolic which capped Canada's Centennial celebrations; a machine which spewed out plastic people with monotonous regularity. It was one way of emphasizing the perils of world overpopulation. Unfortunately, in real life more and more people find that they have to conform in their daily life to a plasticized world. Not so at Armbro. The winner's touch includes surprising margins for individuality.

George Cowan was setting out with his wife to visit neighbours one evening when they saw a black cat. Moments later they saw another black cat running in front of the car. Cowan recalls, "I said to my wife that we had better go home. But she laughed at me and so we went on and, do you know, nothing did happen!" Cowan is seldom so easily dissuaded. There never has been a Number 13 Armbro truck. There may be nineteen sewer crews at work, but you'll never find Number 13. There may be scores of pieces of equipment representing an investment of millions. The men and equipment may be there as a result of the intense effort which has been put into winning a major contract. But if it's a Friday—and horror of horrors—Friday the thirteenth, then it's no day to start a new job. A backhoe may sneak in on Thursday night and dig a little-bitty hole and

15

surround it with some snow fence. That will be enough to assuage the evil spirits and work can proceed normally on Friday morning. Otherwise, the equipment will remain idle and the men will find other things to do.

"Thirteen pieces of equipment, now that's a valid thing," says Cowan. "I wouldn't say I'd deliberately remove a truck if I had thirteen on the job but I would sure look around to find a water truck or something to make it fourteen!"

The winner's touch also includes taking pride in a job well done. But sometimes government specifications make it difficult, if not impossible, to do a good job. The engineering specifications for Highway Number 10 north of Brampton required, for the most part, the same strength in the north and the south lanes. An eminently reasonable conclusion for the planners at Queen's Park. But arrant nonsense to a simple man like Elgin for whom common sense is one of the finer virtues. "They made us build the pavement the same in every lane, but all the heavy traffic is in the south lane carrying aggregate towards Toronto; in the northern lane it's just cars and empty trucks," Elgin says. The planners did not allow for the juggernauts with their almost incessant multi-ton loads. To make a bad situation worse, the northern lane has two miles of experimental pavement. "I'm glad they put it that side. It wouldn't have lasted three days of heavy traffic. Even so, I knew that that experimental pavement wouldn't stand up to even light traffic. I made the government put up signs which made it plain that any break up was due to their experiments and not to our men."

The winner's touch includes encouraging an *esprit de corps* that involves the latest Italian immigrant who has just stepped off the plane from Italy. It comes from having foremen and superintendents who have proved their worth on the job. Part of it comes from having the best equipment available. Canada may pride herself on having a classless society but there is no snobbery so withering as that of construction workers who see a rival company working with inferior equipment. If a man is behind the wheel of a truck ten hours or more every day, the efficiency and the appearance of his vehicle have a tremendous effect on morale. The Armbro truck drivers know that their vehicles have all the heavy duty optional extras plus some options which are unique to Armbro vehicles. As Miss Jean Brodie in her prime would say, "The *crème de la crème*"!

16

Peel Construction has been a major segment of the Armbro complex. Stuart Gardner, general supervisor of sales engineering for International Harvester says, "You might say that our truck suspensions are designed up to the Peel level. Many of our modifications and improvements were first installed on Peel trucks." Significantly, Don McKinnon, who is czar of Armbro construction equipment, began his career behind the wheel of an Armstrong truck. Yet another truck driver, Willard Corrigan, moved on to become superintendent of construction of the runways at the Toronto International Airport and now supervises construction of complex, rein-forced-concrete bridges and overpasses.

Frank Gill is one of the exceptions. An engineer, he was lured away from the Ontario Department of Highways. Gill may use the very detailed physiographic maps of Ontario to find gravel. The detailed, county soil surveys and aerial photography may help to locate possible aggregate sites. Locating aggregate draws on the skills of several disciplines. Also, a little bit of luck can help. There are times when even the most dedicated detec-tive work fails to locate the badly needed supplies in a location which will be economic. One day, none of Frank Gill's antennae had located gravel. Gill sat in the car gloomily discussing the problem with Ollie Somerville, the general superintendent of pits and quarries who began his life with the Armstrongs driving a tractor, building dirt roads. Ollie tells the end of the story: "And then down the road on a bicycle comes a lad who says to us, 'If you're the men who are looking for gravel, my daddy has a gravel pit.' So Frank and I went down and signed him up!"

On another occasion construction superintendent Earl Reid was looking for a "borrow pit"; this is an area from which fill can be taken for construction. Reid made an agreement with a conveniently located farmer. When the surface material was scraped away, Reid found that he had dis-covered the perfect quarry. It is now an ideal source of aggregates for the Ottawa area and it is a modest gold mine.

Then there's the personal touch. Lloyd McIntosh is a mechanic who has worked closely with Ted Armstrong over the years. Earlier, McIntosh had worked for other Ontario contractors. "With the other companies we knew the foreman and maybe the superintendent but never the managers or owners. it gives you a good feeling of confidence to be working along

17

with Ted modifying new equipment so that it works better than ever." Or, as Ollie puts it, "Being part of a family affair has meant a lot to me."

Conn Smythe has seen yet another facet of Elgin. "I don't think there's anything that Elgin can't do. He can even be a diplomat. I can recall his patience in bringing together the most impossible and aggressive firebrands and reaching an agreement. You can only go as far in this world as the men who are holding you up on their shoulders. Ted is the unsung hero, he's one of the best possible men to have at home base."

The winner's touch includes the ability to drive a hard—but not ruthless—bargain. Elgin knows that a friendship can be more profitable than one more turn of the screw. Most of his deals are shrewdly negotiated and profitable. But seldom, if ever, are they one-sided. He may be strapped for fill to complete a construction contract. When he has obtained all the supplies he wants, he may leave behind an ideal site for a baseball park for the town.

The qualities which combine to make the winner's touch are many and various. The phrase which comes to mind for most of his associates of many years is "Elgin's a gambler." But this is an oversimplification. It is more a manifestation of the incredible confidence Elgin has in his own ability and the ability of his companies to perform. In others it would appear like the brashness of a braggart. With Elgin it is just a simple matter of fact. A faith that all will be well in the end.

A long-time minister of agriculture and some-time premier of Ontario was also the member of the Ontario Legislature for Peel County. Colonel Tom Kennedy could be a good friend at court. But Elgin declined to contribute to Kennedy's election campaign. "Why should I pay? I only get the highway work when I'm the low bidder." That sort of matter-of-fact attitude allowed him to sleep at night when the patronage and graft of the Ontario Highways Department surfaced in the 1950s. Elgin carried on undeterred. Some other contractors were rushing round like beheaded chickens, fearful lest skeletons be rattled from their closets.

The winner's touch also involves a single-minded approach to achieving goals. In the beginning it was sheer necessity, in order to survive. Later, it became a habit. While money did not change Elgin's essentially simple, rural tastes, it did tend to compensate for some of the things which

18

earlier poverty and subsequent hard work had denied him. I asked him one day, when I caught him in a reflective mood, whether the standardbred stable actually made a profit. He turned to me, with a look of amazement on his face, "But how could it be a hobby if it didn't pay?"

If you have Elgin for an opponent or a competitor, don't ever prematurely count him out. He makes mistakes, but seldom repeats them. "Wouldn't it be wonderful to know that you were never wrong?" mused Jack McArthur following a conveniently forgotten disaster.

Again, the winner's touch includes the countryman's rude good health. As I have noted, in the whole of his working life Elgin has never been sick for more than a day until he had his eye operations for the removal of cataracts. His health is such that he has always found it difficult to understand how other people can get sick; such weaknesses must not be allowed to intrude on work!

Remembering friends and kindnesses is also an important part of the winner's touch. Many people in all walks of life have cause to be thankful for the Armstrongs' long memory. Pres Graham of Cambridge, for many years a competitor of Mrs. Victoria Armstrong in the hackney show ring, comments, "No matter what venture Elgin got into, it always seemed to make money for him. But he never lost a friend in the process. No matter whether it was a jockey, a harness-racing driver or another millionaire, it didn't make any difference; a friendship made was never forgotten."

It has become something of an anachronism to find a privately owned company which is unionized and in which the workers will go to almost any lengths to bale the boss out when a job goes bad. Elgin says happily, "I have the most loyal organization of high-calibre men that anyone could wish for."

Chapter 3

THE DERRY WEST FAMILY FARM

WHEN Elgin retired from active management of the Armbro companies in 1973, Canada was very different from the country in which he had been born seventy-six years before, on the Derry West family farm. To be precise, Lot 14, Third Concession, east of Hurontario Street in Toronto Township. This has now become part of one of Canada's fastest-growing municipalities, Mississauga. Elgin was the eldest of four brothers, of whom Harold and Ernest are now practising dentists.

For many countries, seventy-six years is not a significant historical era. But Canada is a new country. Those years span most of Canada's social change and economic development. We Canadians tend to be a pragmatic, self-effacing people. We tend to see our growth and development in terms of other countries, particularly the United Kingdom and the United States.

But Canada is a large and bountiful land. It has a lot more going for it than colourful Mounties and Niagara Falls. Nature was particularly lavish to a land of some twenty million people. Canada is one of the significant farm countries of the world. While Canada's exports are dominated by the hard wheats and feed grains of the prairies, the diversity of farm production is unequalled. There are the vineyards and the peach and cherry orchards. There are cigarette and cigar tobaccos, and such speciality crops as ginseng. There are pedigreed seeds from a wide range of forage crops and certified seed potatoes which go to many parts of the world. Your morning boiled egg in England or your exotic chicken dish in Tokyo could both have begun with Canadian poultry breeding. Canadian Holstein-Friesian dairy cattle have been exported to over fifty countries, where they are renowned for their production and longevity. Latterly, Canada has led the world in the development of Europe's exotic beef breeds which had not previously been exploited. We grow popcorn and canning corn, fresh sweet corn on the cob and grain corn for our poultry and livestock. We grow soybeans and the ubiquitous white beans which are baked and shipped around the world with Mr. H. J. Heinz's smidgen of pork.

The great newspapers of the United Kingdom and the United States are realities because of the forests of Canada and our pulp and paper industries. We have a corner on the world's supply of uranium, molybdenum, nickel and potash. Lead and copper, zinc and coal, oil and gas are all harvested from Canadian mines and wells.

Our industrial plants produce diesel locomotives for New Zealand's railways and the uniquely Canadian all-terrain vehicles for exploring and exploiting the Arctic. The industrial outpouring is as great as one's diverse daily needs. But the bustling cities, the productive farms and mines, are still only a small part of this big country. Much of it is quiet and empty. There are the mountains and the tundra, the barrens and the craggy coasts. Why have we let the world see us as a handful of plaid-jacketed lumberjacks and Mounties in scarlet tunics, locked in a land of perpetual snow? This emphasis on the forests, the Mounties and the snow, to the exclusion of so much else, distorts the picture of Canada. The tremendous potential is being achieved in many fields, and at the same time the rugged and unique grandeur of the land is being preserved in huge tracts of National Parks.

So vast a land has enormous transportation challenges. It was the building of the Canadian Pacific Railway which made the prospect of Canada a practical reality; Elgin's Irish mother, Jennie Cheyne, and his Scottish father, Thomas Elgin Armstrong, were then still in their youth. The whole economic, social, farm and urban complex of Canada is now tied together with railroads, transcontinental highways, international-status airports and networks of radio and television which link the Atlantic

21

and Pacific coasts and the United States border in the south, and the Arctic in the north. We also do more talking to ourselves than most countries—that is, if the statistics on the telephones per capita are reliable guides.

In 1897, when Jennie Cheyne Armstrong gave birth to Elgin, none of this existed in Canada. The Chinese had come to help build the railroads and the people of many European countries had embarked on a new life in Canada. But most of the immigrants came from England, Scotland and Ireland. It took special privation and bleak prospects in one's native land to set sail, like the impoverished Irish, for Canada. It meant the prospect of a six-week voyage in infected and ill-provisioned lumber ships returning to Canada in ballast— with people. For some, the odds were too great. Their ill-conceived ventures were ended by dysentery or typhus at such places as Grosse Île in the St. Lawrence River, below Quebec. In a corner of this now beautiful little island is a marker which records the graves of some eleven thousand typhus victims who reached Canada, in vain.

The polyglot Canadian population had earlier received an infusion with the arrival of the United Empire Loyalists from the eastern United States. From the western United States came the Mormons to settle in what was to become the province of Alberta. The vigorous and imaginative campaign for immigrants lured Doukhobors and Ukrainians from Russia, and Icelanders, Poles, Austrians and Hungarians by the thousands. A critic of the times wrote: "The attempt to lure our fellow countrymen to this desolate, sub-Arctic region is to be denounced as criminal."

The odds were infinitely more favourable in Toronto Township where the Armstrong brothers grew up and in neighbouring Chinguacousy Township where the Armbro companies have prospered. (Chinguacousy Township was named after Chief Chinguacousy, the son of a Scottish army officer and a Chippewa mother, who commanded Indian and militia forces in the War of 1812.) This is the "Banner County" of Ontario; Peel County is thought to have been named after Britain's great parliamentarian, Sir Robert Peel. Brampton, the county seat, earned its name from the town's namesake in Cumberland, England, where some of the earliest settlers had come from. The name was thought to have more decorum than the original Buffy's Corners which the settlement was first called, after a popular

22

tavern. Canada is still a young country; Elgin's life has spanned over three-quarters of Brampton's first century.

When Elgin was born, the breadbasket of Canada was not the prairies, but Ontario. Chinguacousy was then one of the big wheat producers; the Armstrong farms even now grow the plump, soft winter wheat for which Ontario is noted.

The early roads were something else again. The heat of summer, the cold of winter and the frost-boils of the spring, when apparent terra firma turned into a quagmire, were among the problems faced by such pioneer Peel County farmers as Thomas Elgin Armstrong. The corduroy roads, with their base of logs from the bush, gave travellers an uneasy ride. The early equivalent of our superhighways were the plank roads. These were made of three-inch planks spiked to sleepers in the manner of a barn floor.

A local historian, Alex McKinney, has divided his life between breeding good Holstein-Friesian cattle, civic affairs and the history of Toronto and Chinguacousy Townships. McKinney's research reveals that shortly before Elgin was born the pioneer roads through the township saw a heavy traffic in wheat and lumber. They were shipped in such volume from Port Credit down on Lake Ontario that the port then took precedence over nearby Toronto. McKinney writes: "The early roads through the township were toll roads begun around 1850. They were built by private companies. The toll was set up at the hamlet of Derry West, which was located a few miles south of the town of Brampton on Hurontario Street." In its prime, just twenty years before Elgin was born, Derry West boasted two churches, a school, a temperance hall, an Orangemen's Lodge and a blacksmith's shop. During the latter half of the nineteenth century it struggled to maintain a post office. Now, Derry West is just a traffic light north of Highway 401.

The plank road which served Derry West ran from Port Credit to north of Snelgrove. The beautifully written minutes of Chinguacousy Township record the purchase of sixteen-foot oak planks, three inches thick, for seven dollars per thousand for the repair of roads. Then the railroad came to Brampton. McKinney continues, "The first train went through on July 1st, 1856 and its whistle killed Port Credit. All the produce from north Peel was diverted by rail to Toronto. Port Credit harbour declined until more recent years when oil companies revived the waterfront. It is interesting to note that for the ninety years up to 1941, the population of the Township of Chinguacousy declined in every census. When the population first peaked, the budget was less than three hundred pounds and forty per cent of these funds came from the twenty-four licensed taverns in the township!"

Around the time of Elgin's birth, early settlers remarked on the similarity of southern Ontario to parts of England, Scotland and Ireland from which most of them had come. Good, cleared land could be had for as little as ten pounds per acre. Appropriately, at the time of Elgin's birth, the Ontario Legislature had passed an act to encourage the breeding of trotting horses. Enlightened legislation had already been passed to encourage tile drainage in Ontario; many parts of the province could only achieve their potential in crop production once surplus water had been removed through intricate systems of tile drains and open ditches. Elgin's arrival on the Ontario rural scene also coincided with the birth of the first telephone associations. Elgin would reach his teens before the first farmer in Ontario had the benefit of hydroelectric power.

As a young boy, helping with the chores on the Derry West family farm, Elgin saw the coming of the era of the internal combustion engine and the automobile. There were then three-quarters of a million horses on Ontario farms and many of them were to be threatened by the arrival of the automobile. The conflict of interest between the horse and the automobile was marked by the introduction of a petition to limit cars to ten miles an hour during daylight and seven miles per hour between sunset and sunrise.

Change is the name of the game. But it is sobering to ponder the changes which have swept the world since the Armstrongs welcomed their first-born at the Derry West farm. The world has gone from horse-and-buggy to moonrockets. The standardbred horses have come from the simple pleasures of the country fair to the wagering of over one million dollars during a single night at Toronto's Greenwood track. Road-building has matured from a farmer's responsibility for maintaining part of his own concession road; now, a single complex, concrete interchange will consume the better part of a farm which once provided the livelihood for a whole family. As a youngster, Elgin was unaware of developments in the dairy in-

24

dustry; a reliable test for measuring butterfat had yet to be invented and the Holstein-Friesian Association of Canada was still not incorporated.

That one lifetime should see such incredible change is a matter of interest. It is a matter of fascination that one person should have influenced so much of that change. From that Derry West family farm were to come Elgin and his youngest brother Ted who were to play so big a part in changing the Canadian scene. They have made major construction contributions to five of Canada's provinces. The success of the Armbro standard-bred horses has put Canada in the forefront of breeding trotters and pacers. The milk yields of Holstein-Friesian cows have increased dramatically. Despite the high average production of milk and butterfat for the breed in 1974, one cow has milk production which dwarfs the rest. Her output for milk is three times that of the average of the breed and the butterfat production is four and a half times! Examine the extended pedigree and there, sure enough, you find the Armstrong touch: that great old cow, ABC Inka May.

Given such prodigious accomplishments, one might have expected a well-documented ancestry for the Armstrongs. However, according to Miss Margaret McLeod, treasurer of the town of Brampton, "Canadian records are incomplete prior to 1927. Registration of births, deaths and marriages has been mandatory in other countries for many years—even centuries—but this was not enforced in Canada until 1927."

The Cheyne side of the family is recorded in some detail. The family tree refers to Luther Cheyne; the 1877 *Historical Atlas of the County of Peel* records that Luther had adjoining farms in the north part of Toronto Township and was a director of the Farmers' Mutual Insurance Company. The Cheynes traced to Scottish and English ancestry, while another branch of the family settled in Ireland in the reign of King James the First. A family Bible, now in the possession of Claude Hamilton of Texas, records that his ancestors migrated from Ireland to Canada, married into the Cheyne family and were buried near Derry West. Perhaps Ted and Elgin inherited their stamina from the Cheyne side of the family. Andrew Cheyne, for instance, sailed out of County Tyrone and landed in New York City fourteen weeks later. Then, with his brother Christopher, he walked from New York City to Toronto, Ontario! The house they built on Huron-

25

tario Street in Peel County in 1824 still stands. Christopher lived to be ninety and his wife Elizabeth to ninety-three.

The authenticity of the family tree as it crosses the Atlantic and stretches further into British history is not so easily established. It's certainly peopled with the characters one would like to have in one's background. There is the sixteenth-century sheriff of the county of Cumberland, and squires who go back to King Ethelred the Unready! There is Gospatric Fitz Arkill, hostage of William the Conqueror, and Arkfrith, a Danish nobleman with extensive land in the north of England: estimable men though they may have been, one hesitates to vouch for them as the forbears of Elgin and Ted. The roots of the Armstrong family are found in the county of Cumberland in northwest England and along the Border Country of Scotland. Sir Walter Scott in his *The Lay of the Last Minstrel* did them justice in these words:

"Ye need not go to Liddisdale
For when they see the blazing bale
Elliotts and Armstrongs never fail."

The Armstrongs' forbears came to Canada from Scotland via County Cork. It was Elgin's great-grandfather who emigrated to Canada. His son Joe continued the Ontario line. The Armstrongs were all strong Orangemen and an Orange Lodge was built on the corner of the Derry West farm. Even Elgin, who is not normally a joiner, is a member of the Orange Lodge and he has taken part in those colourful Twelfth of July parades which celebrate the Battle of the Boyne.

The most impressive structure on the original Armstrong family farm today is the Peel County courthouse. The farm ran to one hundred and twenty-five acres; the additional few acres were added by Elgin's grandfather who traded them for a bottle of whisky. The Armstrongs grew some clover, alfalfa and wheat. The main income came from a flock of one hundred Oxford ewes. There were also a couple of milk cows which provided milk for the family while the male calves were fed on milk and sold for veal.

"It was a pretty serious life," recalls Dr. Harold Armstrong who is four and a half years younger than Elgin. "But we didn't think much about it in that way then. We lived just like everyone else in the neighbourhood.

26

Everyone on a farm was expected to work and contribute to the well-being of the family."

Viewed from an era of automobiles, snowmobiles, television and a night club down on the highway, farm life at the turn of the century might appear mundane. But it had qualities which later generations have obviously yearned nostalgically for. There was no party line telephone then, but everybody knew everybody else's business. There was involvement in church and school. There were the bees when neighbours arrived miraculously to help someone in trouble. Neighbours were the stuff that survival was made of.

From the vantage point of a hundred-horsepower tractor and a chain saw, the days when it was horse power, aching muscles and an axe might look harsh and bleak. But that's not the way Elgin recalls the Derry West farm.

"I was very close to my dad. He was an exceptional horseman who knew how to shoe and gait a horse. We never had much money but we always had a few good horses. I mind the time, when I was maybe ten or twelve, and I'd come home from school and jog one of the standardbreds. The carts were nothing like the racing bikes of today. They had great big wheels with wooden spokes."

The standardbreds were not the élite, pampered creatures of the 1970s. They provided the power to take the family to market or to church. They also had the stamina to pull a plow. There were two pacers. Maud Ellis was a balky animal which Thomas Armstrong managed to train into a racehorse, of sorts. There was also Lady Elgin and a third standardbred which Elgin recalls with particular affection. "I came back from school one day with the prize list for the Woodbridge Fair. I found Dad plowing with the hollow-back-horse. Dad didn't need much persuasion and we jogged our way to Woodbridge with the hollow-back-horse . . . and won the race."

Thomas Armstrong, with his flair for handling standardbreds, took King Jubilee, a colt owned by his uncle-in-law, George Cheyne, to Bolton Fair. The skittish colt made a break when some of the excited crowd surged onto the track. King Jubilee, with Thomas Armstrong on the bike, came back to win the free-for-all. He raced two further heats. This infuriated George Cheyne who thought his horse was being overtaxed. Cheyne left the

27

fair in anger and drove his buggy twenty miles back home. Undeterred, Elgin's dad went on to win four heats. This gave King Jubilee such a local reputation that he was sold to a Toronto furniture dealer for six hundred dollars; a tremendous price for those days. He went on to compete in the Grand Circuit. The furniture dealer provided a legacy of five hundred dollars for the burial of his horse on the Derry West farm and maintenance of the grave.

Thomas Armstrong had two studs. There was Golden Jubilee who matured into a popular stallion and Golden Rule who was a thoroughbred sire. Thomas would take Golden Jubilee, either in the shafts or trotting behind the cart, as far afield as Georgetown to breed mares. The usual stud fee was fifty dollars.

Few British people could tell you the date of Queen Victoria's birth. But, as all Canadians know, it is celebrated on May 24. It's a time of year when the country needs a celebration. The long, cold winter has been finally shrugged off. The crops are in the ground and the warmth of summer is only a whisper away.

May 24 was a good time to take the sheep down to the Etobicoke Creek and wash them in preparation for shearing. Perhaps it was the heat generated by chasing some uncooperative ewes or maybe it was the cold water of the creek which had only recently thawed. Anyway, Thomas got chilled and contracted tuberculosis. He was never again able to cope with the farm chores.

Elgin's youth was to be short-lived. He went to the one-room Broddy school where the education was rudimentary and the sports limited. Elgin remembers playing soccer but it could not have been a very sophisticated game because he hasn't the faintest idea of the positions on a soccer team. But he does recall "I used to score most of the goals, because I could run pretty fast in those days."

School absenteeism because of chores and haymaking began to show. Elgin failed to pass the geography and history exams. His formal education ended with just four years of schooling. He was a graduate of Grade 4 and in charge of the family fortunes. Tuberculosis had sapped the last of Thomas Armstrong's strength. Elgin, at fourteen, became the family breadwinner.

28

Elgin Armstrong

The parents of Elgin, Ted, Harold and Ernest Armstrong pose with members of the Cheyne family. Front row from left, Thomas Elgin Armstrong, Grandfather George Cheyne, Mrs. George Cheyne, James Cheyne and Mrs. Thomas Elgin (Jennie Cheyne) Armstrong. Back row from left, Mrs. Andrew Cheyne, Uncle George Cheyne, Andrew Cheyne and Mrs. James Cheyne.

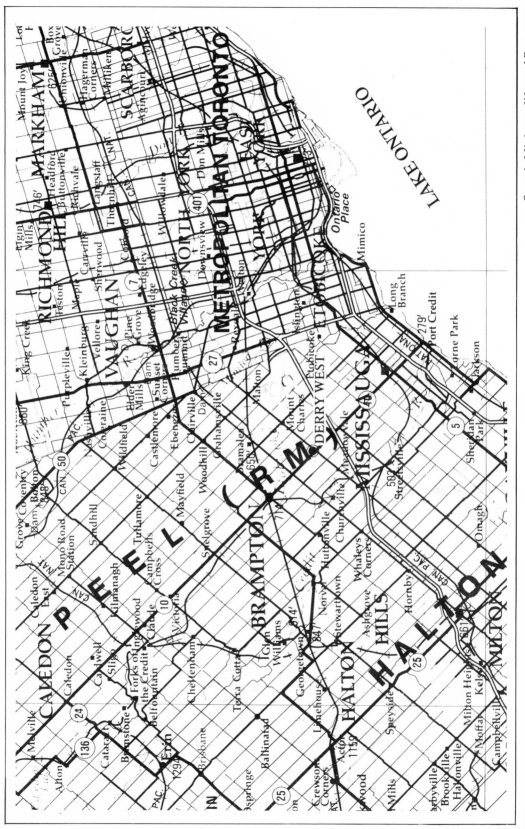

LAKE ONTARIO

Ontario Ministry of Natural Resources

An elevating grader conveys dirt to horse-drawn, bottom-unloading wagons; this is the way Ontario's roads were built in the year when Elgin and Ted entered the construction business.

It was 1929 and rippers and scrapers and caterpillar tractors were nudging the horse aside; coincidentally, it was the year Elgin and Ted formed their partnership and also the year of the great crash on Wall Street.

The Armstrongs began to earn their first nickname, "the dirt movers of Brampton."

George Cowan

Caterpillar tractors were used to haul a train of earth movers and were filled in sequence by an agile operator—no job for the accident prone!

International Harvester Company

Elgin, the entrepreneur, poses with the nucleus of the fleet of International Harvester Company trucks. They are IHC A Line models and the year was 1930.

Brothers Ted (left) and Elgin Armstrong flank the latter's son Charlie in the tack room at Brampton.

Elgin first got the feel for road construction when a blend of horses and horsepower was typical.

Globe and Mail

Victoria Armstrong with some of the more than 10,000 trophies won by the ABC hackney ponies.

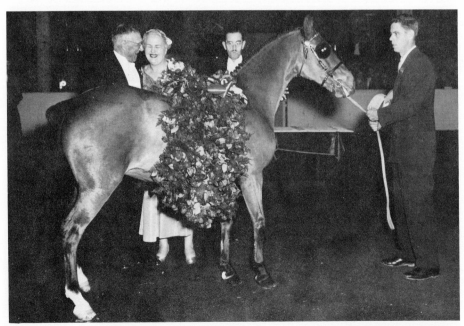

Canada Pictures Limited

Colonel Tom Kennedy, former Ontario Premier and long-time Agriculture Minister, congratulates Victoria Armstrong at the retirement ceremony for Crystal Lady at the 1954 Royal Agricultural Winter Fair in Toronto.

The stylish Crystal Lady takes Victoria in a viceroy around the exercise track at ABC Farms

Elgin's My Kingdom wins the 1955 Sussex Stakes at Goodwood, England, in an exciting photo-finish.

Michael Burns

(Top) Jockey Hugo Dittfach scores a runaway victory in 1965 with Ouzo at Wood-bine. *(Below)* Ouzo in the winner's circle with, from left, trainer Art Warner, ABC Farms Manager Dr. Glen Brown and Charlie Armstrong.

Turofsky, Toronto

Elgin's daughter Mary (Mrs. Geoff Holly) receives the Clarendon Plate at Old Woodbine from Ontario Jockey Club **Director** J. M. Macintosh. At right is trainer A. J. Routcliffe and jockey C. Fonte who had a muddy ride aboard Heptad.

Carl Klein photo

Black Velvet soars over the hurdles at Buffalo, New York. The high-flying gelding was named for the **Armstrongs' original Black Velvet** which was Victoria's dowry along with a Holstein cow.

Ted Armstrong set up rock-crushing and aggregate plants in many parts of Canada; this one was part of the wartime work in Newfoundland where the Armstrong brothers built gun emplacements.

Construction of the causeway across the Barrington Passage linking the mainland of Nova Scotia with Cape Sable Island was nearly financial disaster for the Armstrong brothers; no rock could be conveniently found in rocky Nova Scotia!

O'Dell and Shields Studios

Holstein-Friesian breeder Jack Fraser was one of the Peel County dairymen whose stock contributed to the foundation of the ABC herd.

Strohmeyer and Carpenter

A group of ABC matrons all of whom produced in excess of 20,000 pounds of milk in a single lactation.

Strohmeyer and Carpenter

Montvic Rag Apple Sovereign, the sire of ABC Reflection Sovereign, was the end product of the tremendously successful Holstein-Friesian breeding of T. B. Macaulay at his Mount Victoria Farms in Quebec.

Strohmeyer

ABC Inka May, the dam of ABC Reflection Sovereign, was one of the great brood cows of the breed. Her conformation won the classification of Excellent and the Grand Championship at Toronto's Canadian National Exhibition; no piker in the production department she produced 24,141 pounds of milk and 1,128 pounds of butterfat as a four-year-old.

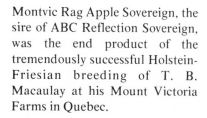

Strohmeyer and Carpenter

Simply "ABC" became enough to identify ABC Reflection Sovereign anywhere in the Holstein world.

Strohmeyer and Carpenter

ABC Shamrock Mildred, an Excellent daughter of ABC, was Grand Champion female in Chicago in 1953, took the top award at the 1955 CNE and passed on the good qualities of ABC to her own progeny.

Canada Pictures, Toronto

Tom Hays sparked the export of Canadian Holstein-Friesians to some 50 countries. One of his South American customers was Hector Astengo of the Argentine who purchased the ABC Holsteins and carried them to even greater plateaus under the Rosafe banner.

Peter Lewington

Elgin never forgets old friends, like banker Jack McArthur whose faith in the Armstrong brothers never wavered—despite the balance sheets. McArthur was honoured by the University of Guelph during its 1974 Centennial Year for his contributions to Canadian farming.

Michael Burns

A thoroughbred mare named More Daisies was the dam of the first Armbro horse.

Chapter 4

THE ENTREPRENEUR

Hard work is a panacea. Thomas Armstrong died in April, 1911, and by Good Friday it was birth which occupied Elgin. "It was the coldest Easter I ever remember. There was a hell of a storm with high winds. That night there were lambs all over the place. You never saw the like of it. I don't know how so many ewes could lamb in one night. The lambs and the ewes got mixed up and I had a big job sorting them out. I remember one lamb that wouldn't suck. I watched and the mother touched him on the tail with her nose. He started to wiggle his tail and then went right ahead and sucked. After that I found that if you tickle them on the tail they think it's their mother and they go ahead and suck . . . unless they're too far gone with the cold." The lambs that were raised successfully to between sixty-five and seventy pounds would fetch some twenty to twenty-five dollars. For three years. Elgin ran the farm with his mother, much as his father had. There was enough for clothing and the necessities of life; but not enough for Elgin.

The seeds of the natural-born entrepreneur and manager of money had begun to germinate. At the age of eighteen, not yet old enough to vote, Elgin talked a Brampton bank manager into backing the largest sheep sale yet seen in Ontario. "I wasn't old enough to sign the note, but they thought I was and never questioned it. I bought six hundred sheep from local farmers and advertised the auction sale in the *Farmer's Advocate*. Sam Mitchell added a carload on consignment. I got hold of Bill Russell, who had a good reputation as an auctioneer. The farmers came from Fergus and all over to buy the sheep! We had a couple of light wagons meeting the trains as they arrived at Brampton Station. We had another wagon to bring them in from Malton in the other direction. We sold $28,000 worth of stock that day. Sheep I bought for $7, sold as high as $25. Some I paid $10 for, fetched $50. I really cleaned up. When all the expenses were paid, I'd made $2,000 clear profit."

Typically, Elgin didn't keep the money for long. He promptly bought another farm of one hundred and twenty acres for $7,000.

Alfalfa, the queen of the forage crops, was beginning to earn its popularity as a high-protein feed for livestock. Elgin concentrated on alfalfa seed production. His biggest yield per acre was fifteen bushels and the highest return was fifty dollars a bushel—although nine to ten dollars a bushel was more customary.

Eastern Ontario has long been known for its export of dairy cattle. Elgin explored the farms in the Gananoque area and returned with a carload of thirty-five Holstein-Friesian cows. "And ten days later I had them all sold for a nice profit. So I bought other cows. I always went for the cows that looked best for production and the sort that would raise a good calf. A few select cows I kept to build our own herd. This was the first time I owned a registered Holstein cow."

Characteristically, Elgin was not dedicated to the cows; when an opportunity came to sell them for a profit, he was ready to explore new ventures. Peel County had heard about sweet clover and "the word was spreading like a house on fire," Elgin comments. But growing seed, any sort of forage seed, can make you very vulnerable at harvest time if you don't have your own equipment. The entrepreneur had learned another lesson: not to be vulnerable. Elgin invested in a clover huller and a gasoline tractor, "so that we could save the seed when it was really abundant. For threshing clover and alsike I charged a dollar a bushel and there was many a day when we bagged seventy-five to a hundred bushels."

This was a time when Ontario farms were worked by some three-quarters of a million Clydesdale and Percheron horses. Most farmers were content to haul the sheaves of grain to storage in the big bank barns which are so much a part of the Ontario countryside. The entrepreneur saw another opportunity for business. There was enough grain to be threshed to keep a custom operator busy from fall to spring. Typically, Elgin bought the biggest threshing machine available. He had added both a Fordson and a Case tractor and also a stationary wire-tie baler. "We then had three gangs going. A clover huller, a grain-threshing machine and the baler. We did such a good job that everybody wanted us to do their work. Price was no object as long as we got there on time and got the job done. Many is the night I worked until 12 o'clock." The entrepreneur had learned yet another lesson which was to be put to good use in later years: a reputation for speed and efficiency was the best possible advertisement.

Meanwhile, the farm work had to be done at home. With two binders, Elgin would get his own crops gathered in safely, before going out to do custom work.

Ted had begun to show the mechanical ability which later was to contribute so much to the Armstrong brothers' success. He worked at an abattoir which afterwards was to form part of the Canada Packers complex. With the prospering custom business, Ted began working part-time with Elgin. Sometimes it was with a tractor and sometimes with the team of big grey wagon horses.

"My first memory of Elgin was his threshing our clover. He did a good job—just like everything else he tackled," says Alex McKinney, whose Chinguacousy Township farm has been held by McKinneys since the days of the Indians.

Threshing sparked the first Elgin memories for Doug Middlebrook. "Elgin farmed beside my dad and I remember him threshing for us. He also did some baling. But he was so hard up he couldn't carry on until we supplied the wire. He's known his tough times. But if he said he'd do something, you didn't have anything more to worry about."

"Elgin had more imagination than the rest of us," is the opinion of Dr. Harold Armstrong. "He was always buying and selling. He was a natural salesman and trader."

Sandy Cowie had joined the Armstrong brothers to operate the baler. Cowie was to remain with the Armstrong brothers during their nearly fifty years of road construction which spanned technology from the horse scraper to continuous-pour paving machines.

31

The flame of competition burns bright in any entrepreneur. Elgin found time to enter oats and corn in county crop competitions. The work horses, when not busy with the custom jobs, could be seen at the local country fairs winning ribbons.

The biggest of all fairs in Canada is the Royal Agricultural Winter Fair, now universally known simply as The Royal. Toronto, with its bigger bankroll, had outbid other cities contending for the fair. Toronto newspapers of the day advertised that The Royal would "reveal the marvels of a winter exposition unprecedented in the history of any nation in the world!"

People came by streetcar from the city and by special trains from the Prairies. The affluent arrived in Maxwells, Durants and Peerless Eights. Schoolchildren got in for a nickel, while the well-to-do purchased six-seat boxes for the duration of the fair for fifty dollars. Entries from nine American states swelled the entries from every Canadian province to a total of 17,000. There were 1,850 horses, 2,500 cattle, 9,000 sheep, 7,000 swine and 9,100 poultry. The normally staid Toronto *Globe* proclaimed, "Royal Winter Fair greatest on earth." The *Toronto Star* hedged its bets with "The best and biggest of its kind on the continent of America, if not in all the world."

It was November, 1922 and The Royal had succeeded, despite other attractions. A dollar bill would buy you Thanksgiving dinner at the Walker House, which still stands catty-corner from its plush neighbour, The Royal York, in Toronto. There was Al Jolson declaring that "I wish I could shimmy like my sister Kate," while over at the Massey Hall, built by the farm equipment fortune, there was none other than Sergei Rachmaninov at the keyboard. At the movies, Rudolph Valentino was vying with Jackie Cooper and Lionel Barrymore.

And there, down at The Royal on Toronto's waterfront, was Elgin, the entrepreneur, competing with his alfalfa seed. In discussing his participation in the inaugural Royal, Elgin recalled how he won. A search of The Royal's archives by John Wiley, executive secretary, revealed a rather different outcome. Eighteen entries finished in the prize money with fifteen dollars for first, and two dollars each for a group in the ninth position. Elgin came in number six and carried home his winnings of five dollars. He was to return in later years, with other members of the Armstrong family,

32

to compete in Holstein-Friesian and numerous horse categories. But meanwhile, there was more pressing business such as getting married and earning a reputation as the dirt mover of Brampton.

Chapter 5

THE DIRT MOVERS OF BRAMPTON

APPROPRIATELY, it was at a barn dance that Elgin met Victoria Lawrence who was to become his bride. Today, a barn is remarkable for its efficiency and also its lack of character. A dull, uniform, steel shell may now provide environmental-controlled housing for poultry or livestock. But the barns of an earlier era were structures of dignity and grace; the greatest soared like cathedrals, with their hand-hewn timbers giving the illusion of the chancel roof. The barn framer, like the blacksmith, was among the aristocracy of artisans. The actual barn-raising was an event in every community. When it was completed, the spanking new barn became host to all who had helped. It was a housewarming as only Ontario knew how to stage. The years to come might see endless, arduous chores; but for one night at the barn dance it was fun. Feet are flying in a merry reel to the tune of a fiddler. And there is Elgin plucking up courage to ask "the prettiest girl I ever saw for a dance."

Victoria was the daughter of Charlie Lawrence, a neighbouring farmer whose family had come to Ontario from England's Somerset. He is remembered as a great horseman who, appropriately, "died in the furrow of a heart attack behind his team." On that summer evening, as Elgin danced with Victoria Lawrence, he found that she was due to leave for a visit to western Canada in the morning. The grass has not been remarkable for its growth under Elgin's feet; he too was on the train next morning.

34

He was part of that pilgrimage which enticed farm boys west for fifty years. It was the annual harvest excursion.

Elgin's destination was Brandon, Manitoba, while Vicky continued westward to her relatives. But on the way, there were splendid courting opportunities. It was an age of both drudgery and leisure. As the train worked its way westwards there were pleasant stops at wayside stations, where the passengers could get out and pick blueberries. The evenings were passed with games of cards.

It was 1917 and the wheat from the prairies was being harvested with horse-drawn binders. Young men like Elgin followed the binders and stooked the sheaves. "We lived in a bunkhouse which had only recently housed chickens. Unfortunately the harvest crew ahead of us had left behind a crop of bedbugs and lice. I took my blankets and slept out in the hay mow. I damn near froze. I didn't get much sleep because of the cold and the cries of the coyotes at night."

The threshing machine was run by a primitive, single-cylinder tractor, which burnt fuel oil and was started with a dose of ether. "But it was very hard to start. To turn the flywheel, we wrapped a rope around it and hitched it to the flat-rack of a wagon. I then drove off with a pretty good team of horses. But they must have put in too much ether. The tractor backfired, tore the rack off the wagon and sent me flying."

The return of Elgin and Vicky to Ontario was celebrated with a fowl supper at Trinity Church. "You know how it is; I was young and excited and forgot my purse," explains Elgin. "I had to borrow the fifty cents from another boy who was there." Later that summer Vicky was suddenly taken ill and was "sent home from the hospital to die." Instead, she sought help from a Christian Scientist and recovered good health which was to last her until shortly before her death in her seventies. The Christian Science religion became a great motivating force in her life.

In the fall of 1918, Elgin and Vicky were married. Vicky's dowry was a good Holstein cow and a beautiful gelding called Black Velvet. They were hardly settled in the Derry West family farm before that wartime, virulent strain of influenza swept the country. Jennie Cheyne Armstrong died and the newlyweds became responsible for bringing up Elgin's three younger brothers. A farmer's daughter, Vicky was used to cleaning out stables and

35

milking cows. In later years she indulged in the expensive hobby of hackney ponies but her apprenticeship with the reins came from necessity. In the spring, she drove Black Velvet hitched to the seed drill. As the summer days lengthened, she drove a team in the hay field.

"As usual, on a Saturday night we'd go into Brampton to exchange our eggs and butter for groceries. We would be allowed fifteen cents a dozen for our eggs and twelve cents a pound for our butter. For a treat, we went into the Green Lantern restaurant for a cup of tea and a piece of toast. I couldn't afford the quarter, but a lady there was reading fortunes in teacups and so we had ours read. She said that I was dealing with a bald-headed man (and I was), that I would become very wealthy, Mother [Vicky] and I would live to a ripe old age and we'd have five children." They were to have four daughters and one son. Helen, Mrs. Malcolm Southgate, worked closely with her mother with the hackneys, and became one of the most successful lady drivers of the show circuit. Mary married Geoff Holley and the Holleys subsequently moved to Florida. Isobel married Bryan Burkart who now heads the Armbro Aggregate Division. Ruth became Mrs. Arscott, while Charlie, their only son, and his wife Lenore, now live with their three daughters on the current ABC farms. That fortune teller's predictions were remarkably accurate.

For the better part of the 1920s, the Armstrongs were all kept busy running the two farms. Most of the farm income came from forage seed production, milk, lambs and horses. The custom threshing continued to prosper. When not working their way through the Toronto School of Dentistry, Harold and Ernie helped with the farm chores. Ted's time was divided between his job in an abattoir and maintaining the farm equipment.

"It was finally decided to sell the farm and the estate was shared between us four boys. I didn't have a clear idea of what to do next. I've always liked growing flowers and considered the greenhouse business." (Brampton is known as "Flower Town," for the profusion of hothouse flowers which are grown in the scores of acres under glass.) "But I decided in favour of the road business because more money changed hands than with the flowers."

Elgin had acquired a taste for road-building from his farm days. "If things were slack on a summer day, we'd take the teams of horses and haul stone from Meadowvale Station. Sometimes I had a scraper behind the team and sometimes we hauled gravel for Peel County roads." When the big Case tractor was not needed for farm custom work, there were always a few dollars to be had grading the roads of Toronto Township. Ted had discovered his talent for repairing and modifying anything mechanical. Elgin had found that he had a natural gift for maintaining a grade, without benefit of a level or stakes.

It was 1929. The ramifications of the First World War were over. The country had recovered from a series of recessions and depressions. The long-cherished hope of Sir Wilfrid Laurier that "The Twentieth Century belongs to Canada" appeared feasible. The business outlook was so promising that Elgin and Ted formed the Armstrong Brothers Company partnership. The ink on the agreement was hardly dry before the Wall Street crash occurred, which heralded the Great Depression.

Allan Barr, who had joined Elgin and Ted a year earlier, vividly recalls the launching of ABC. "On the strength of a contract for hauling gravel in Dufferin County, Elgin bought six Chevrolet trucks. The Chev trucks had no cab and we'd have to sit on a box over the gas tank. The power was so low and the Dufferin County hills so steep and inclined to be sandy that we could only carry loads of one cubic yard! Total capacity was one and a half yards—we have loaders today with ten-yard buckets! Anyway, even with a load of one yard, we'd have to go down the hills wide open and even reach fifty miles an hour. That was tops for those little four-cylinder motors and certainly put a lot of stress on the wooden-spoke wheels. All I can remember of Elgin on that first job was his incessant, 'Tramp on her, boys!' " Elgin had begun to build his reputation as a fast worker and the dirt mover of Brampton.

Dump trucks were then something of an innovation. They were competing in Dufferin County with farmers who were drawing gravel with teams of horses and gravel boxes loaded by hand. By the time the farmers had made one trip, those Chev trucks had made nine. Allan Barr, who was an avid reader, taught himself how to replace bearings and pistons in the rudimentary motors. Often he'd work long into the night maintaining the trucks.

37

The fledgling construction company got forty-five cents per yard for the first mile, sixty-five cents for two miles' haulage and eight-five cents for a three-mile haul. The Dufferin County job was completed ahead of schedule. Elgin and Ted had a profit of fifteen thousand dollars, which was promptly invested in earth scrapers and a sixty-horsepower Caterpillar tractor.

Farmer Russell Morrison had joined the team. "In those days you went out to make money for the fellow you worked for. You knew he couldn't have you around unless he made a profit. We couldn't afford anyone who was just interested in dinner time and payday. It was all just like working on the railroad. Construction gets in your blood; we enjoyed the dust, the excitement and the travel. Some of our construction work was so much of a novelty to country people that they would gather on the banks of the highway at night to watch. Normally, we would start at 5 A.M. and run right through to 9 A.M. Sometimes we'd work on into the night. Then our crew of eight men would stagger off to a nearby farm where we boarded; it would soon be 5 A.M. again."

One of those people sitting on the side of the highway was Stan Smith, who was eventually hired. Smith is rated as a good mechanic, stubborn as a mule and, according to George Cowan, "the strongest man I ever had anything to do with." Smith points out that "ABC was ahead of any competition by using rippers, scrapers and graders in highway construction." And then, unconsciously, he put his finger on the ingredient which enabled the company to prosper: "*We* built the highway."

Sandy Cowie had worked with Elgin and Ted threshing grain and grading township roads. Now, he too was captured by the excitement of road construction. Charlie Armstrong recalls Cowie as "a perfectionist. If you didn't pay attention when you were backing up your truck to the shovel, he'd dump the gravel and then pick up the end of your truck!"

From day one, the Armstrong brothers seem to have attracted the workers who were to stay with them. It certainly wasn't due to the perquisites. Elgin says, "A working day was from daylight, often till after dark. We usually worked eighteen hours a day and I always maintain six hours' sleep is enough for any man. The boys were willing to work because they got good wages and big paycheques. They'd quit at four o'clock on

38

a Saturday so that they could go home for the weekend. Sometimes I'd run the scraper or the grader, but I always had a couple of extra men around to spell the boys off on a hot summer's day."

They had a good team. Men like Pete May who, after many years in construction, went on to manage the farm which earned world renown for both horses and Holstein-Friesians. By the time they got their next big contract in Oxford County, ABC had ten stalwarts. "All of them farm boys," Elgin comments, true to his theory. "I very seldom got a guy out of the city who was any good. They just wouldn't stay. They'd make a big splash and then leave you. It was the rural boys who stayed with you in construction."

Elgin had that happy knack of separating physical and mental work. While he was grading, he would be thinking of where the company should be in five or ten years. He'd be figuring out how to swing a deal on new construction equipment; he always wanted the biggest and the best even when he didn't have a nickel in his jeans.

He had decided to be a contractor instead of a subcontractor. ABC built twenty-eight miles of Oxford County roads and went on to become a familiar outfit across Ontario. Then, in order to get some provincial work, Elgin broke his own cardinal rule and went back to subcontracting. The experience cost him eight thousand dollars, when the contractor failed to pay his debts. And that was enough to put the overextended ABC enterprise just one jump ahead of the sheriff.

Chapter 6

ONE JUMP AHEAD OF THE SHERIFF

"**N**EVER lend money to a man who runs a custom threshing machine, preaches or travels a stud horse" T. R. McLennan, manager of The Royal Bank at Paisley, Ontario, was fond of advising youngsters like Jack McArthur, who began his banking career as a clerk in a country bank. Elgin is not given to preaching but he did have a stud horse and he did have a threshing machine!

Not the best omens for a young man looking for credit in a business noted for its large credit needs and high incidence of business failure.

"Many times I'd thought of Elgin as a fool, but he always had the habit of coming out right. He has great imagination, good timing and good judgment," his brother Harold declares. He was to need these and other qualities in order to survive the awesome depression of the 1930s.

Not that Elgin ever recognized that there was a depression. He was soon doing contract work for four levels of government. There were township and county roads to be built and maintained. There was some work to be had with the Ontario Department of Highways, as the provincial government sought to stave off the debilitating effects of the depression. Elgin and Ted got their first federal paycheque when they worked on the Welland Canal, linking Lakes Erie and Ontario. By the summer of 1930, they had graduated to building a complete section of highway in the Paris-Galt area of Ontario, now known as Cambridge. This involved the building

40

of roadside ditches, installing drainage culverts, making the road bed and surfacing it with gravel; in those days it was customary to surface even a major highway with gravel, spray it with asphalt, and delay paving for five or six years.

And so it went; the Armstrong Brothers Company (ABC) signs became a familiar sight across the length and breadth of Ontario. How was it that two Ontario farm boys, with scant education and no special advantages, succeeded when all around them there were long lines of unemployed, and established companies going into receivership?

"From spring to freeze-up we worked long hours and got maybe five dollars at the end of the week for groceries. In the winter, we plowed the snow and when the equipment broke down we'd spend a chilly night in a barn. And there were Elgin and Ted working right along with us," George Cowan remembers. And then George, almost in an aside, drops the clue which gives us understanding from the vantage point of the welfare society of the 1970s. "But it was always fun!" That the Dirty Thirties should be recalled as "fun" by someone who eked out an existence is due in large measure to Elgin's *modus operandi* and sense of humour.

Cyril Clark, Peel County farmer, municipal politician and cattle drover, has known Elgin since the day in 1925 when Elgin threshed a crop of his clover. "Elgin was always very energetic; if he hadn't been, he wouldn't be where he is today. He always tried to do a good job and that's what made him prosper in the road business. But money and success never changed him," Clark says.

There was a strong instinct for survival which became evident when Elgin's continuous and enthusiastic expansion was threatened by the failure of a contractor who owed ABC. When the company was hanging on the ropes, not just the owners, but also the dedicated workers pitched in by day and night to make ABC a success. Everyone did visibly productive work. There was no room for those highfaluting engineers and pencil-pushers who then rated very low in Elgin's scale of priorities. If a man wasn't working a shovel or driving a truck, he just couldn't be working! The miniscule records of the thirties compound the problems of biography. However, the recollections of the Armstrong veterans vividly show that it was a decade when the company hovered on the brink of bankruptcy.

Ollie Somerville is a barrel-chested man with biceps like a young maple tree. He is the very epitome of a construction worker. He has graduated from driving a tractor to supervising the work of all Armbro pits and quarries. To Ollie, Elgin was "such a quick man. If he saw an opportunity he would be after it so fast that he had it out from under you before you knew what was going on!"

But in over two years of interviewing people who have had business and social contacts with the Armstrongs for fifty years, no one has ever suggested that he was too sharp. Elgin never went for the jugular and the last drop of blood. He always left his opponents some room to manoeuvre. Both old colleagues and adversaries were left with the feeling that they were dealing with a master chess player who had figured out the next several moves.

He also had the ability to relax. George Cowan recalls many days when they would drive away from Brampton on a long trip to hunt up work. George would find that Elgin's thoughts had turned to farming or to horses, and then, to the chagrin of George who is a compulsive worrier, Elgin would be sound asleep.

Phil Doucet, sometime Brampton barber and a member of the non-Establishment legion of Armstrong friends, remembers: "Even when ABC was faced with financial disaster, the problems of the company were never allowed inside the home. It was the strong will of Victoria Armstrong which kept business and the problems of the world outside."

Elgin acknowledges this debt. "I was away a lot and it was Mother [Vicky] who developed our really closely knit family. We never had any serious family disputes. In fact, the only arguments we ever had were over horses."

Elgin's own philosophy is littered with deceptively simple clichés and the sort of homilies which would never fall from the lips of professors who teach business administration. But the Elgin technique works. It's all a matter of "Watching things closely." And "Using good judgment." Success hinges on "Bidding the job at the right price and getting it done ahead of time."

The planning included snow-plowing contracts. That way the heavy equipment overhead was defrayed the year round, and the nucleus of good workers could be kept on the payroll.

42

The Elgin style has always been marked by a belief that machines, no matter what the horrendous price tag, were cheaper and easier to find than good men. "Even when I didn't know how I'd meet the payroll, I had extra men. That way we kept the machines operating. It also meant that the work carried on, even though we went off to estimate a new job or look at new equipment."

The single-minded pursuit of success also had its limitations. There was almost no involvement in the children's education, community affairs, good works or municipal politics; the pursuit of enough money to keep one jump ahead of the sheriff was what the Dirty Thirties were all about.

Bill Willis went on to build his own construction equipment company which supplied some of the major pieces for the Armbro companies. But in 1932, when Bill Willis was installed as ABC office manager, his job was to protect the ten-thousand-dollar investment of Mickey McMurchy, one of Elgin's few sleeping partners. The ABC equipment was then stored on what is now Brampton's municipal parking lot on California Street; every time there was a spring flood on the Etobicoke Creek, it would be under water. Beside the lot, a small concrete block building still stands; very few modern pieces of construction equipment could even be manoeuvred through the doors. But then it was big enough for Cheyne Edwin Leroy, better known as Ted, to tinker with any malfunctioning equipment.

Down California Street and across on Main Street was the old Haggert Block. And there, in a rented room above the butcher's shop, Bill Willis wrestled with the ABC accounts. "The books were in horrible shape. Elgin owed the International Harvester Company, the tire company, and even some of the machinery had been repossessed. He was in danger of being cut off from other sources of credit."

"It was not so long ago that the Armstrongs couldn't cash a two-dollar cheque on the Main Street of Brampton," according to the accountant of an equipment supply company. Phil Doucet remembers that "Elgin was refused credit for some picks and shovels at one of the two hardware stores. But he's not a small man. When his fortunes were restored, he divided his business between the two stores."

Elgin and Ted picked up a little work building or maintaining farm laneways. The returns were minimal because the farmers were harder hit than most segments of society by the depression. Bill McCaugherty, who was later to sell Elgin some of the foundation animals for the renowned ABC Holstein-Friesian herd, remembers a comment by Elgin: "I've got half the equipment dealers in Peel County out hunting up work for me!"

Some, like International Harvester, never wavered in their faith. There were instances when Elgin was not able to place an order, but IHC executives would start the production line rolling because they were sure that somehow Elgin would come through.

They probably didn't know just how shaky the whole business was.

"During the depression years we had to make one licence plate do for each two trucks. When we went through town we'd drive close together, in the hope that no one would notice," says Allan Barr. In contrast, the changes in truck licence fees and provincial gas taxes in the 1972 budget added over one hundred thousand dollars annually to the cost of operating the Armbro companies; the increase in the cost of gasoline in 1974 added well over one dollar per hour to the operation of every dump truck.

In the early thirties the Armstrongs couldn't afford their own aggregate equipment or a pit. They operated from a pit owned by Jack Parr, near what is now the intersection of Highways 7 and 10. Today, some of the most sophisticated aggregate equipment in the world is working at the several Armbro pits in the area; but then, according to Allan Barr, "We had a small tractor-driven crusher. One winter, we dug back into the stockpile of crushed gravel to load the trucks by hand at Parr's pit. Suddenly Elgin shouted, 'Get out!' Sure enough, the frozen shell of gravel above us had started to cave in. It all came crashing down and we were lucky not to be buried alive."

The Armstrong brothers unwittingly compounded their own problems by the speed of their work. Frequently, jobs were finished ahead of schedule, long before the government involved had completed its estimates. The provincial government, for instance, made up its estimates every thirty days—and thirty days was almost too much for a company hanging by a gossamer financial thread.

It was not long before McMurchy and Harold Armstrong had had enough. "We loaned ABC two thousand dollars because Elgin was too strapped to get any of the trucks licensed," Harold Armstrong reminisces.

"Then, to our astonishment, we learned that Elgin had used that two thousand as a down payment on fifty-thousand-dollars' worth of new equipment. That was the end for me. I couldn't stand that sort of gamble and feared that I'd be sucked in, and swallowed up!"

ABC nearly went under on that Highway 5 construction job at Cambridge. The highway engineer, through an oversight, had not completed his estimates on time. Only frantic telephone calls to Toronto and a wild ride to Cambridge with a cheque staved off the creditors.

Unflappable Elgin recalls complacently, "I always kept my credit in good shape. You know, there are two bad things you can do with your financial obligations. One is to pay in advance and the other is never to pay."

Chapter 7

THE WAR YEARS

Tᴴᴱ late 1920s and most of the 1930s had been a rugged apprenticeship for Elgin and Ted. With the outbreak of World War II, they had the nucleus of a key group of construction workers and the expertise for more than moving dirt.

A factor in the defeat of the Axis powers was the success of the Commonwealth Air Training Scheme. Young men from all over the Commonwealth—130,000 of them—came to Canada to learn how to fly. They were joined by the Free French and young Dutchmen who fled the East Indies to equip themselves to fight the Japanese. The Armstrongs built many of the needed airfields. Some have been restored to crops and others have grown to become commercial airports.

Just about everyone in Canada seems to have an Armstrong anecdote. A southern Ontario sheep farmer goes fishing in Manitoulin Island and spends the evenings swapping yarns with Armstrong workers who live at a Manitoulin farm while building a highway. The blacksmith who shoes horses at the Windsor raceway remembers how Elgin got gas on credit at the corner gas station north of Lucan while he was building the Centralia airfield. "He let Elgin have gas on time because he trusted him."

For years Earl Hooper, of St. Marys, Ontario, had one of Ontario's finest Holstein herds. "When the Armstrong brothers were building Centralia airfield, it was one of the places I added to our milk route. We'd go

46

anywhere in those days to sell milk. Money was as tight around Centralia as it was anywhere else at the end of the depression. I remember that Imperial Oil was ahead of us in asking for money from the Armstrongs."

With years of construction experience—primarily road-building for various levels of government—Elgin and Ted were naturals to get contracts for building runways. The runways were really more like roads; they were built on a base of crushed rock, the area was suitably drained and the runways were surfaced with dirt. The first airfield was completed by the end of 1940 at Alliston and returned a profit of $10,831.02.

And so began what amounted to a flying circus. Arifields were laid out at Deseronto and Goderich, at Hamilton's Mount Hope and at Port Albert and Mountain View. In all, some eighteen airfields were built for use by the young men of the Commonwealth.

For some, the war meant ravaged homelands, privation and death. While many Canadians served and fell in the war, and the country made significant contributions to the Allies' cause, there was a great deal on the other side of the ledger. The war lifted Canada out of the depression of the thirties; as wartime contractors, the Armstrong brothers were major beneficiaries.

"In the early days of the war when we were building Centralia Airport, there would be three to four hundred people hovering around the site looking for work; one and a half years later we didn't have anyone left between nine and ninety! Then, we began taking on people who were even warm, in an effort to finish a job," is the way George Cowan saw the transition. Charlie Armstrong, who is now vice-chairman of the board, went off to join the forces. Bob Charters, who now holds down the president's job, was hiking his way over the Pyrenees, having been shot down over France.

To complete the Sky Harbour Airport, north of Goderich, ahead of schedule, Ted had designed and built a grader forty feet wide. He put together mobile cookhouses and the forerunner of today's mobile homes. But there was a difference. They were built to last. Some would go to Newfoundland and back and some would still be in use after twenty years of abuse.

In the cook shack would be Don Campbell. His training as a cook was on a par with all ABC training for just about every manual, mechanical or executive position; he began as a truck driver. While Campbell is remembered with affection, his cooking is not. Ted says, "He had one cake mix and a different cake every time. He had one pie recipe and a different pie every time!"

Despite the stream of government contracts, Elgin and Ted remained in precarious financial straits until 1943. They then vacated the base in the heart of Brampton and bought the nucleus of ABC Farms, at the junction of what is now Number 7 bypass and Highway Number 10.

Ted Armstrong and Ollie Somerville were learning how to crush rock for the apparently endless runways and roads. "It took us two and a half weeks to move a crushing plant, even though the output was just three hundred tons a day. Just a fraction of what we now crush in plants at Caledon and Bovaird's pit," says Ollie. "Sometimes stones as big as cannon balls would fly thirty feet or more out of the crusher. Nobody wore a hard hat in those days; our heads were supposed to be hard enough."

The company grew. ABC spawned Peel Construction, to be followed by Montcalm and a dozen more. And then, says Ollie, "By God! We got a contract in Newfoundland."

The ubiquitous U-boats had penetrated the Gulf of St. Lawrence. Twenty Allied ships were sunk, no fewer than nine by U-517 and her captain, now Admiral Paul Hartwig. The convoy taking Armstrong men and equipment from Montreal to St. John's was attacked and three boats were lost en route to their first assignment, which was to protect the magnificent harbour of St. John's. Across the bay from Signal Hill, gun emplacements were to be built at Cape Spear. That meant first crushing thousands of tons of rock to build the road from St. John's out to the cape. In retrospect, the rock-blasting techniques seem not only crude but more hazardous than being in the front line against Hitler. Two men would swing their sledgehammers in easy rhythm as the third rotated a steel bar. Once a hole large enough to hold the dynamite had been made, the explosive charge was tamped down the hole. One powder man was even more venturesome than most, and Ted was obliged to have him work in a corner of the quarry away from anybody else. Only just in time, as "We soon had the gruesome job of gathering him up in washtubs."

Today, when explosives are moved along the highway there is usually a police car fore and aft and prominent warning flags. Not so in Newfoundland, which was suddenly seeing more activity than at any time in the history of Britain's oldest colony.

"There were three of us crowded into the cab of a truck taking dynamite from St. John's out to the cape," recalls Ollie. "There wasn't much room in the cab and we must have jiggled the hoist lever. When we got out to the cape we found that our truck, which had no end gate, was empty. We had laid a trail of dynamite all the way out from town."

Even Ted got a little careless and set off a charge large enough to hurl a sizable rock right through the wall of a nearby home. "A girl came out screaming, 'You've blown the leg right off my dad!' We warily went in to take a look and were relieved to find that he still had two legs, but only one trouser leg!"

That wasn't the only confrontation with the people of Newfoundland who had lived an incredibly insular life, relieved largely by the visits of explorers and fishermen over the centuries. There was nearly a riot when Elgin tried to pay the men in paper money. No flashy paper money for them! The standard item of currency was still the twenty-cent piece.

Now, one wonders how the Allies won the war. Those weeks of rock crushing culminated in the arrival, from Singapore, of sixteen-inch naval guns weighing thirty-five tons apiece; guns which might better have been left for the defence of Singapore. They were loaded on wagons at St. John's wharf, and the cavalcade left town only to have the wagons collapse and the guns fall into the muskeg. After prodigious effort, they were dragged to Cape Spear and installed. It was perhaps as well that Hitler never came to call because the guns could only be brought to bear by hauling away on ropes.

The runways at Gander Airport had to be extended and there were sundry contracts at Phillip's Head on the Bay of Exploits. Over on the west coast, at Corner Brook, the Armstrong brothers were facing the special problems of maintaining construction crews thousands of miles from home. A badly needed compressor, loaded on a forty-ton flat car flew off at a curve and months later was located and retrieved from the muskeg. Then there was that most famous train, with its history of linking the extremities of Newfoundland; the *Newfie Bullet* set new records for the days that it was delayed by heavy snow, the winter the Armstrongs spent in Newfoundland.

49

There was a special sadness too. Godfrey Cook who joined the Armstrongs as a foreman in 1929 and went on to become a job superintendent, was flying back to Montreal aboard a Liberator. "We had completed the three gun emplacements and were returning for other wartime contracts. But then, by radio, we were alerted to look out for a plane down in the Atlantic. We searched in vain for five hours." Sir Frederick Banting, the co-discoverer of insulin, was working on aviation medicine at the time his plane went down en route to England. A great Canadian had been lost, without a trace.

As the war dragged on, the Armstrongs built army camps in Ontario and airfields in Nova Scotia. They excavated for a Halifax hospital in Nova Scotia and contributed to the building of the veterans' Sunnybrook Hospital in Toronto.

There were the first big contracts for developing Toronto's Malton into its present international airport status. There was also a $14,000-contract with the Township of Toronto which returned a gross profit of $32.52—before deducting depreciation, general overhead and maintenance.

Gun emplacements had to be built on the north shore of craggy, beautiful Cape Breton Island. A major project was the building of gun emplacements to protect Halifax, Canada's major east coast port, for the convoys making their perilous journeys back and forth across the North Atlantic. A suitable shoal of material for aggregate was located at Lawrencetown, beyond the eastern passage. Ted set up his crusher below the cliffs and Elgin built the railroad to take the aggregate to Dartmouth. At that time there was no bridge linking the twin towns of Dartmouth and Halifax and the last leg involved a ferry.

As if to emphasize the urgency of the work, a U-boat shelled the crusher, and a passing Greek grain freighter was torpedoed. The Greek survivors were brought ashore, and promptly the daughter of the crushing foreman, Earl McGugan, went down with diphtheria. "She was a beautiful little girl and she was dead by morning. We always thought that the Greek crew were carriers of the disease," Elgin says. "Fear of the disease was such that we couldn't get an undertaker and no hospital would take the other McGugan children into quarantine. We built a coffin ourselves and used a truck as a hearse and the boys as pallbearers. We buried the little girl in the cemetery and the only person to come was a local preacher who read the burial service."

After four years of intermittent work on the Atlantic coast the war-time contracts faded. By 1946, the gross—not the net—profit had slipped to sixty-four thousand dollars. Then, Elgin landed a construction plum. The Nova Scotia government, afte years of petitioning, had finally decided to build the Barrington Passage Causeway linking southern Nova Scotia with Cape Sable Island. (This was an isolated community of a few hundred people and not to be confused with Sable Island where, more recently, oil explorations could lead to boosting the economy of the Maritimes.)

Any causeway needs the strength of rocks of massive dimensions. The Barrington Causeway was no exception because it jutted out into a storm-tossed part of the North Atlantic. The Nova Scotia Department of Highways had done the research and located suitable rock stretching down ninety feet. Not that anybody really thought such research was necessary; Nova Scotia is largely rock.

This was one of Elgin's first really big contracts. He posted a certified cheque for fifty thousand dollars as security and ordered a fleet of equipment which was shipped from Ontario and Quebec.

Cape Sable Island was separated from the mainland by just three-quarters of a mile; but the channel was thirty feet deep and noted for its fast current. Innumerable five-ton chunks of rock would be needed to stem the erosion of the ocean. But, to Elgin's astonishment, there was no rock to be found in rocky Nova Scotia! It transpired that the test drills had penetrated a rock formation which was shaped like a duck's egg; but all around it there was no rock suitable for the causeway. To go to other parts of the province in search of rock would have made the project prohibitively expensive.

"As the contract had been tendered on the basis of the provincial government's rock research, I telephoned the minister of highways and told him there was no rock. 'Too bad,' he said. 'You've got the contract and we've got your cheque for fifty thousand dollars.' Now, it was their responsibility, because they didn't do enough testing. It had already cost us thousands of dollars to retrieve a two-yard shovel which had sunk in what was supposed to be our quarry."

Within three hours Elgin had called the minister's bluff. To the chagrin of the people of Nova Scotia, who had long awaited a causeway, the equipment was loaded for shipment back to Ontario and Quebec. Feeling sure that Elgin was in a bind, the province's chief engineer and the provincial premier had looked at the site and with a casual "We've got your cheque," they went off on a fishing trip from nearby Yarmouth.

Elgin never reads a book and his writing seldom exceeds the confines of a package of Marguerite cigars. But he knows the power of publicity. "The people had wanted that causeway for forty years. It would help the export of crab and lobster to the United States. Failure to build the causeway would be a hot political issue. I made sure that the newspapers got the full story before we pulled out."

The Armstrong reputation had not been built on welshing on a contract. If they felt they couldn't complete the job, then nobody else was likely to bid.

"We got as far as Trois Rivières in Quebec and holed up there with the equipment. It wasn't long before the Nova Scotia Department of Highways wanted us to come back and renegotiate a contract. They did some more drilling and found some rock close enough for us to finish the causeway. I'd figured it was better to lose that fifty thousand dollars than to stay with an impossible contract; but it took a lot of nerve to pull out."

Because of man's profligate overfishing of the oceans and wanton pollution, the once profuse lobsters of Nova Scotia are now just a gourmet luxury. Most restaurants bring their lobsters all the way from South Africa. But for the Armstrong men, who built the causeway, lobsters became a staple diet. There was a continuous boil of lobsters and a "mug-up," as the Nova Scotians refer to their incessant cups of tea. The building of the causeway somehow symbolized the contrasts in a changing way of life in rural Nova Scotia. The steel for the causeway was hauled to the site by teams of oxen which were rented by Elgin for a dollar a day.

Finally, the Barrington Passage Causeway was finished. Elgin, halfway across the two-lane highway to Cape Sable Island, was greeted by the premier of Nova Scotia. The Armstrongs' Atlantic construction was at an end, the war was over and they headed back to Ontario; back to something which had lapsed during the depression and the war years. Elgin was a dairy farmer again. This time, he was to change the Holstein-Friesian breed and make ABC even better known for cows than it was for construction.

Chapter 8

A STAR IS BORN

THE complex ABC Holstein-Friesian story has its roots in Canadian and United States history and involves cowmen and company chairmen, promoters and politicians. ABC breeding can now be found in just about every Canadian herd and in every corner of the globe. Like all complex stories it has no neat and tidy beginning and it apparently has no end. But none of it would have happened without a long distance telephone call.

It was five o'clock on a February morning in 1946 when the telephone rang in the farm home of Tom Dent; it was a telephone call which would change, for the better, the Holstein-Friesian breed across Canada and around the world. A roadside statue at Woodstock, Ontario, commemorates the feat of Dent's cow, Countess, the first Canadian cow to exceed a lifetime production of two hundred thousand pounds of milk. Dent's herd sire was even more famous and his service was being requested by phone.

Tom Dent (then a member of the Ontario Legislature) was the proud owner of Montvic Rag Apple Sovereign.

"Sovereign"—the Man of War, the Secretariat, the bull of all bulls— was a son of Emperor of Mount Victoria and out of Montvic Rag Apple Colantha Abbekerk, a cow capable of producing nearly thirty thousand pounds of milk with over four per cent butterfat in a single lactation; she was a brood cow noted for passing along her attributes to outstanding progeny. And, in the third generation of the pedigree, was Johanna Rag Apple Pabst, the most influential Holstein bull in North America for type conformation and butterfat.

Cliff Chant, herdsman of ABC Farms, had telephoned Dent to alert him that a vial of semen from Montvic Rag Apple Sovereign would be needed; ABC Inka May, the Armstrongs' best brood cow, was in heat.

"I badgered Elgin to let me breed Inka May to Sovereign but he protested he couldn't afford the hundred-dollar service fee. But I kept after him every time he came to the barn. Finally, he relented and said 'Well, you're so damn persistent! O.K. I'll get the money some place.'

"Sure enough Tom had the semen ready for me, as promised, when I drove into Woodstock. I put the little vial of semen into my shirt pocket to try and keep it at body temperature; the use of frozen semen was then many years away. I jumped back in the car and raced to Brampton to breed Inka May." Unknown to Chant, he was involved in the biggest, single happening in three centuries of the black and white cattle in North America.

The Armstrongs were to continue the breeding of modern Holsteins as they became the world's premier breed; there was a time when our Holsteins were referred to disparagingly because of their production of "blue milk." T. B. Macaulay, president of the Sun Life Assurance Company of Montreal, set out to change all that. He aimed his sights at breeding high-producing cows with good-quality udders—and four per cent butterfat. He was not just another wealthy man dabbling in cattle breeding. His study of genetics ranged from plant to animal breeding. He had had practical experience with Shorthorn cattle and Canadian Cattle, a Quebec aberration.

Johanna Rag Apple Pabst came to Macaulay's Mount Victoria Farms following a successful fifteen-thousand-dollar bid at auction. Convinced that Johanna was a prepotent sire par excellence, Macaulay used him heavily and followed him with his sons, grandsons, great-grandsons and even a great-great-grandson. The purchase of foundation brood cows was equally felicitous. From the 1920s, for two decades, the Abbekerks, the Megs, the Bonheurs, the Pietjes and the Hartogs dominated the Montvic herd. And it was all under the management of a great cowman, Mort Butchers, who was at Mount Victoria for the entire development of the Rag Apples.

55

Even before heading the Montvic herd, Johanna had been selected
All-American champion three times; twice he had been Grand Champion
of the National Dairy Show and had received the judge's nod at Waterloo,
Iowa and other major exhibitions in the United States. In 1927, he was
made Grand Champion at Canada's Royal. He came back to win in 1929
but his show days were largely over; he had more important work to do at
home.

Throughout the 1930s, his progeny dominated the show rings in North
America. Numerous offspring also excelled in production; Montvic Rag
Apple Colantha Abbekerk became a world champion of butterfat production. Every tested daughter of Johanna averaged in excess of Macaulay's
target of four per cent butterfat.

Cattle breeding can be a slow and discouraging business. Macaulay
was among that handful of breeders since the days of Robert Bakewell who
lived to see the success of their work. Shortly after Macaulay died in April,
1942, the Montvic herd was dispersed. The opening bid of $6,500 for a cow
topped the sale, which was remarkable for the consistently high average
prices. In spite of wartime gasoline rationing and scarcity of car tires,
people came from several Canadian provinces and many parts of the
United States for one of the greatest buying opportunities in history.

The Holstein-Friesian Journal of August 1942 noted: "You can trust
Tom Dent of Springbank Farm, Woodstock, Ontario, to do good buying
and he lived up to his reputation when he purchased the April bull calf
Montvic Rag Apple Sovereign at $4,075 for himself and Clark E. Brown
also of Woodstock. While this is the highest price paid for a calf of this age
in many a day, he is an 'Emperor' son of the World's Champion Butterfat
producer and Canadian National Exhibition Grand Champion Montvic
Rag Apple Colantha Abbekerk."

While the popular, prolific and prepotent dairy sires grabbed the
headlines, Elgin knew the worth of good brood cows and bought the best as
the foundation of the ABC herd.

"It is quite an accomplishment to breed one brood cow who leaves her
mark on the Holstein industry. Therefore when one man breeds nine great
brood cows he should be asked to stand up and take a bow. Douglas S.
Dunton, Glenvue Farm, Brampton, Ontario, please stand up." So began a

well-deserved tribute in *The Holstein-Friesian World* of June 10, 1962. One of those great brood cows was Inka May whom Cliff Chant had seen in heat and wished to breed to Sovereign. "ABC Inka May was the All-Canadian four-year-old in 1947 and she made 24,141 pounds of milk and 1,128 pounds of butterfat that year. She is the dam of four sons, one Excellent and three Very Good," noted the *World*.

By the fall of 1946, Inka May was heavy with calf. But, momentarily, a different aspect of birth occupied Cliff Chant and his wife Mabel. A Brampton cinema was showing an educational movie on parenthood. Queen Victoria had long gone to her reward but Canada had still not quite shaken off the Victorian era. The men went to the movie house one night and the ladies on another!

Cliff saw that Inka May was close, but he didn't think she was that close to calving. He reluctantly went to the movies, with the promise that Mabel would call the theatre manager if Inka May went into labour. "The show had nicely started when they paged me and I went right home."

But it was Mabel who was the midwife at this prestigious birth. Cliff Chant was greeted by the sight of Inka May licking and nuzzling one hundred pounds of wet and wobbly-kneed, black and white calf. A star of the Holstein world had been born. ABC Reflection Sovereign was to make an even greater impact on the breed than his illustrious forbears, such as the great Johanna.

"ABC Reflection Sovereign was the most influential sire that ever lived," according to Chant. But he may be biased; how do others see him?

Roy Snyder, now general manager of the Ontario Association of Animal Breeders, who was in on the ground floor of Canadian artificial insemination, says, "In several ways he has continued to exert a major influence on the breeding of Canadian Holstein-Friesians. There are now very few bulls without ABC blood. ABC Reflection Sovereign is the foundation of modern Canadian Holstein-Friesians. There has not been another like him and we don't have another on the horizon."

Tom Hays, who pioneered the export of Holsteins, comments, "In 1946 I spent days and weeks trying to buy Inka May from Elgin. I had an offer from Chile which I didn't think he could refuse. But Cliff Chant told Elgin 'If you sell Inka May, you're going to have to get a new herdsman!'

So that stopped me. I knew that Cliff was doing a great job for Elgin and now I'm glad that I failed to buy her. I don't think we'll see a herd like ABC again."

Chapter 9

GETTING IT ALL TOGETHER AT ABC

"I aimed at having the best Holstein-Friesian herd in the country for production and type. I emphasized both. I wanted production to pay the bills but you have to have type too." An ambitious target for anyone's lifetime; but for Elgin it was largely accomplished in just six years.

This time, when Elgin got into the dairy business the odds were more in his favour than in the days when he scoured eastern Ontario for heifers which would make him a buck. When the Armstrong brothers relocated their construction yard in Chinguacousy Township in 1943, some four hundred acres made the nucleus of ABC Farms. Real estate values were rather different then; one of the first hundred acres was purchased for just $6,600. While the Holstein herd was in existence, there was a strange anomaly in Elgin's financial affairs. The Armstrong Brothers Company had grown beyond the wildest expectations of Elgin and Ted. But they were still cash-poor, primarily because Elgin regarded any success as a springboard to further expansion.

As with every other endeavour, the ABC herd was built on people. Pete May, the farm boy who was part of the shoestring Armstrong Brothers Company throughout the depression years, became the farm manager and was in his element. When he later visited New York's Madison Square Gardens his comment was, "Well, wouldn't that hold a pile of hay!" Pete May put the Armstrongs back in crop competitions and Elgin recalls: "He couldn't have farmed better if he'd owned the place." Throughout the years of the ABC herd, Cliff Chant remained herdsman. He had come from the herd of George M. Clemons, who had decided to disperse his own good herd when it seemed that cattle breeding conflicted with his duties as secretary of the Holstein-Friesian Association.

By the 1940s Elgin had the cash or a line of credit—which in his mind were indistinguishable—to buy the cattle he wanted. He picked the brains and the breeding of some of the best people in the business: neighbours like Doug Dunton, Jack Fraser and Bill McCaugherty. Because some of these Peel County herds had been using bulls of similar breeding, the ABC herd really became an extension of breed improvement which people such as Dunton had been striving for since the 1920s.

The Ontario Department of Agriculture used to sponsor dairy profit competitions. Prizes were awarded for the largest net profit for a cow or heifer which had not been previously entered in the federal government's milk-recording program, Record of Performance (ROP). The forerunners of today's highly successful Dairy Herd Improvement Associations (DHIA) were the cow-testing organizations. One of the first to operate successfully was the Peel County Milk and Cream Producers Association, which began milk recording as early as 1922. This was the starting point for Doug Dunton who was to go on to become president of the Holstein-Friesian Association, a type-classifier and a judge of dairy cattle respected whether the show was in Canada, the United States, Australia, Mexico or South America. "I was farming with my dad and we had all sorts of grade cattle; some dairy Shorthorns, some Jerseys and some Guernseys. None of them gave enough milk. So when I got married in 1927, Dad and I formed a partnership and I went out and bought my first purebred Holstein. She gave more milk than any other three cows in our herd at that time. We selected on the basis of milk production and butterfat and good functional type, only to lose our herd with tuberculosis in the 1930s."

When Doug Dunton began rebuilding his Glenvue herd he got some seed stock from Lorne Davidson who had long been testing his cows. "I was looking for heifers which would develop into good-looking animals with serviceable udders. Not deep udders; I never wanted a cow with a deep udder, because I felt that that was a serious fault. To me, a good breeder does it from the neck up; records are a good guide but you have to use good cow sense."

And a little bit of luck. Two of the early herd sires left their mark. Inka Supreme Reflection, mated to Temple Farm May, led to ABC Inka May and ABC Reflection Sovereign. Incidentally, Temple Farm May, rated as a Very Good, two-star brood cow, was sold to Elgin in dam for just four hundred dollars. The other early sire at Glenvue was Strathaven Top Grade. His progeny included the Excellent cow Glenvue Nettie Jemima, an eye-catching cow, who gave birth to five Excellent sons.

Jack Fraser's Spring Farm was also involved in the formation of the ABC herd. The links between Spring Farm, Glenvue and ABC can be seen through the bull Spring Farm Inka Jewel, whose Excellent son was none other than Inka Supreme Reflection. But Jack Fraser is among those cattle breeders who like to emphasize the importance of good cow families. Fraser's eye for cattle was to take him to the top of the Holstein-Friesian Association and around the world judging his favourite black-and-whites.

The pattern of bloodlines extended to the herd of Bill McCaugherty who had a good herd of Holsteins founded by his father. "Doug Dunton and I bought bulls from Jim Henderson of Kingston; both of them were sired by Spring Farm Inka Jewel. There was a bloodline running through the herds of Jack Fraser, Doug Dunton and my own."

Leslie Purkis, one of the federal government's more experienced ROP inspectors, first tested the ABC herd in July, 1945. "I was pleased to find some of the foundation cows had come from the herd of Bill McCaugherty. These were descendants of Spring Farm Nig Palmyra. I had first tested his daughters in the McCaugherty herd back in 1940 and had a very high opinion of them."

The involvement of the McCaughertys with ABC is just pure Elgin. McCaugherty says, "My dad had dug wells and drilled wells all his life and we were still short of water. I carried on the unsuccessful search and then decided I'd go where I could see the water running. I thought if we could put in a bypass from the creek and filter the water we could then pipe it up to the barn. I telephoned Elgin for an estimate and he was down the next day.

61

"Cliff Chant came down with him and somehow we got talking about heifers. Elgin inquired the price and I told him $250 apiece.

" 'Done. I'll take them.'

"Well, I was taken aback with his speed of decision and asked how many he wanted."

Elgin looked at him with some surprise and said, "Why, the lot."

"As Elgin was preparing to leave, I reminded him that he hadn't come to buy cattle but to estimate on a water installation."

" 'Oh! I forgot,' said Elgin and pulled out a cigar pack, which had adequate room for any calculations he ever wished to do. He had the cost of water diversion, a filter system, a pump house and two thousand feet of pipe figured out in seconds.

"It was all done so damn fast it would make your head swim. The next day he had the pipeline in and the whole job was finished the following day. Even then Elgin had a lot of men working for him but he knew the name of every darn one and exactly what job they were on."

As the ABC herd took shape, it looked more and more like a Peel County herd with a great deal of similar breeding. "But as with any newly established herd, there were also a lot of cattle with different bloodlines," recalls Doug Dunton. "The best of them went on to great things and the rest disappeared."

Disappeared like the progeny of Spring Farm Pathfinder whom Elgin calls, "The worst counterfeit I ever saw! I had about thirty heifers from him and sold the lot. I found I'd made a mistake and unloaded, quick."

A combination of good breeding and ruthless culling meant that a collection of Holsteins became a herd. Tom Hays saw them as "good cattle with size, scale and good udders. Elgin had an eye for pedigrees, he had the right people to work for him and advise him, and he also used his own good judgment. I can't recall any herd developing in so short a time."

"I was trying to get in quick and fast with a good class of cattle," is how Elgin remembers the formation of ABC Holsteins. But he was also preparing for the day when he might sell out. When the Hays boys decided to disperse their herd and go into marketing Holsteins, and anything else from polar bears to rabbits and swine which showed the prospect of profit, Elgin saw the chance to buy a headliner for sales' bait.

One cold winter's night Harry Hays spied a likely cow at Didsbury, Alberta, and Alcartra Gerben joined the Hays herd. Alcartra Gerben was milked four times a day. As a five-year-old she put up 27,745 pounds of milk and 1,409 pounds of butterfat. The test was a whopping 5.8 per cent, enough to give Alcartra the world record for butterfat production. Not bad for a cow which Harry Hays paid two hundred dollars for.

When the Hays' herd was dispersed in 1947, the value of Alcartra had appreciated to eleven thousand dollars—primarily on the aggressive bidding of Elgin. Ted and Elgin had picked up Cliff Chant to go down to the Hays' sale in Toronto. "I thought we were just going to watch, because we had plenty of cows back home. I realized that the bidding was awfully close to me. I looked around and realized it was Elgin. I said, 'My God man! You can't bid on her, we don't want her at all.' "

Chant feared that the world record, made at a time when the exigencies of war drastically reduced the number of tests, could not be duplicated. As a four-year-old Alcartra Gerben had only tested 3.72 per cent and her daughters were not remarkable butterfat producers. "When we got her home, I tested her privately and couldn't get a test above 3.5 and 3.6 per cent. I never put her on ROP test again. She had the record and nobody could take it away from her."

The purchase of Alcartra Gerben was at such variance with the way in which the rest of the herd had been painstakingly assembled from three herds of similar breeding that the cynics felt she was purchased for promotion. Elgin smugly comments, "Alcartra Gerben was the best advertising we ever had. Her world record helped bring in buyers from North and South America."

The Holstein-Friesian Journal has been the Bible of the breed under the editor Hugh Colson who has put out every issue since Volume I, Number 1, in April, 1938. The May, 1943 *Journal* has a brief note that the Armstrong brothers of Brampton had bought some cows from the Canadian Pacific Railway supply farm at Strathmore, Alberta, when its herd was brought to Markham, Ontario, for dispersal. The April, 1948 issue pictures ABC Reflection Sovereign for the first time and he is identified as "our junior sire." In the months that followed, the ABC ads drew attention to the Excellent grading won by ABC Inka May. By June, 1948, ABC was featuring the number of cows which had exceeded twenty thousand pounds of milk in a single lactation. Next, the daughters of Inka Supreme Reflection were featured, and by August ABC Farms had appropriated the inside cover for full-page ads. The September issue gloated over the ABC triumphs in female honours at the Canadian National Exhibition. The November, 1948 issue extolled the virtues of Doug Dunton's two great brood cows, ABC Inka May and Glenvue Nettie Jemima, and their impact on the ABC herd.

The January, 1949 issue had something of a bombshell. ABC had sold out lock, stock and barrel to Hector Astengo of the Argentine.

This is how the ABC advertisement appeared:

ANNOUNCING THE SALE OF A.B.C. FARMS

Six years ago we started in a small way to breed and develop a Holstein herd. At that time we had no idea that A.B.C. Farms would receive the appreciation it has from breeders of Canada and throughout the world. It has been a matter of great pride that we were able to develop so many high record cows and show winners.

It is with mixed feelings that we now announce the sale of A.B.C. Farms and Holsteins to Mr. Hector Astengo of Rosario, Argentina. Although we have known him for only a short time we already hold him in highest esteem—a man of high principle, integrity and keen sense of humour. We believe the future development of the herd could not be entrusted to better hands.

We worked hard and did the best we could but we firmly believe that you will see a better farm and greater herd under the new name of Rosafe. Mr. Astengo is an experienced Holstein breeder and a keen student of pedigree. We certainly wish him well.

Inasmuch as this will be our last opportunity to speak as owners of A.B.C. Farms and Holsteins we wish to express appreciation to Cliff Chant and Pete May for the conscientious and excellent job they have done for us in developing the herd and farm. We are indeed pleased that it is Mr. Astengo's wish that the same staff will carry on in their present capacities. It is our earnest hope that the new owner may enjoy the same profit and pride of ownership that has been our good fortune.

And now, to the many friends we were able to make during our happy experience as Holstein breeders, thanks for everything and good-bye.

Elgin & Ted Armstrong.

Also in that issue was Hector Astengo's announcement and the reference that the ABC prefix would be replaced by Rosafe. (Astengo coined this from a combination of the city of Rosario in the county of Santa Fé in the Argentine.)

INTRODUCING A NEW NAME

ROSAFE FARMS

Mr. Hector Astengo of Rosario, Argentina, is pleased to announce the purchase of A.B.C. Farms and Herd from Armstrong Bros. Company. The same management will continue—Cliff. Chant as herd superintendent and Pete May as farm manager. Every effort will be made to further develop the well-known A.B.C. Holsteins.

In future the farms will be known as Rosafe Farms, the same name as used by Mr. Astengo for his holdings in Argentina. The Holsteins bred by Mr. Astengo in Canada will carry the prefix "Rosafe".

A TRIBUTE TO ARMSTRONG BROS. AND STAFF

Seldom have we seen farms in as fine condition and as perfectly maintained as A.B.C. at present. This also is true of the buildings, equipment and great herd. We congratulate Armstrong Bros. and their staff and we pledge ourselves to continue what has been so well founded.

To our fellow breeders in Canada we extend Greetings and look forward to a continuance of the good fellowship we have already enjoyed so much.

ROSAFE FARMS, BRAMPTON, ONT.

The broker who engineered the transfer was none other than Tom Hays of Hays Farms International Limited. Bill Watson who headed The Royal for years after a distinguished agricultural career, once introduced him at a Royal York dinner with the comment, "Tom Hays may not be the first man on the moon but he'll sure be the first one there selling Holsteins."

"We were doing a large business with the Argentine and in 1946 we first sold some Holsteins to a fellow by the name of Astengo. He then had some seventeen thousand beef Shorthorn cattle and had bought the best bulls from the Perth, Scotland, sale. He was a complex man of Italian parentage. He spoke Spanish and also excellent French, which was just as well as he had a mistress in Paris. By September, 1948 he was looking for a farm in Canada because he wanted a place safe from the Peron regime. He wanted a farm and a herd of cattle which he could operate for ten years and then disperse as the best herd in Canada. I told him that there was only one herd that I knew of that could get the job done and put him on a world basis in just ten years. And that was the ABC Farms.''

Such a sale would provide the capital needed for the postwar expansion of Armstrong Brothers Company. While Elgin had made a big play in buying Alcartra Gerben, he was still making payments to Hays! After those years of being one jump ahead of the sheriff, Mrs. Victoria Armstrong had got a taste for the stability of ABC Farms and was already involved with her very successful, showy hackneys. She refused to agree to the sale of most of the farm and all of the Holsteins, and it took all the blandishments of Elgin and Tom Hays before she finally conceded at four o'clock one morning. Later that day Astengo took possession.

That is the most likely sequence of events. But not nearly as interesting as the several apocryphal versions which still go the rounds. One such version features a chance meeting of Tom Hays and Astengo on an airliner returning from South America. Hays parlayed that chance conversation into a ten-thousand-dollar fee according to "unimpeachable sources." Equally sincere eyewitnesses said, "We were attending a horse show at Madison Square Gardens in New York when up came a chap who turned out to be Dr. Astengo."

Jack Trepanier was, and still is, solicitor for the Holstein-Friesian Association of Canada. "I got involved at the instigation of the secretary, George Clemons. Astengo's French was bad, my French was worse and George Clemons contributed some bad Spanish in our effort to converse on the sale of ABC Farms." Being a good lawyer, Mr. Trepanier has a copy of a draft agreement drawn up on December 10, 1948.

Elgin has the last word on the sale of ABC to Hector Ignacio Astengo. "I was showing Crystal Lady at the Chicago Livestock Exposition. She won her class and Chap Carter, our trainer, drove her round the ring while the band played 'O Canada.' A stranger followed Crystal Lady back to her stall and approached me. 'Are you Mr. ABC?' He didn't even know my name! He was obviously familiar with Holsteins and referred to an ABC-bred bull in South America. He told me he liked Canada and wanted to buy a farm there. So I said, 'I'll sell you one.' I made a snap decision and priced the farm at $225,000 which was the price that we got.''

But that wasn't the end of ABC—it was only the beginning.

Chapter 10

ABC BECOMES A LEGEND

T HE lucky few in public life whose affectionate nicknames become household words have achieved that indefinable extra asset which sets them apart from the crowd. When ABC Reflection Sovereign became known throughout the Holstein fraternity around the world simply as "ABC" he too had achieved such status. ABC Reflection Sovereign had become a legend.

Officially, ABC died on July 1, 1957. Seventeen years later his progeny were fetching record-breaking prices simply because their dams were "by the immortal ABC."

No matter whether the herd is owned by a wealthy industrialist or a farmer-breeder, the cornerstone is ABC: herds like Romandale and Almac. Stephen Roman, with his lucrative interest in Canada's largest uranium mine, was able to build a herd without regard to expense. The foundation included daughters of Lonelm Texal Highcroft, ABC Reflection Sovereign and Spring Farm Fond Hope. Wherever possible, all the females were bred to ABC. Through the use of ABC, Romandale was able to win the show mantle which had been first won by the ABC herd and passed on to Rosafe. The Almac herd of the McIntosh family of Oxford County was also built on ABC blood. The result was a herd with 90 records averaging 17,362 pounds of milk and 600 pounds of butterfat.

The Holstein-Friesian Association of Canada, which cannot afford to play favourites, concluded in the 1970s: "ABC Reflection Sovereign is the greatest Canadian Holstein sire of all time." Bill McCaugherty used to enjoy going up to the ABC barns to see how his heifers were developing. He recalls ABC as a "big bull; a wonderful rump on him, good depth of heart and good springing ribs all combined to make him a good-looking dairy bull."

The unique stellar-status of ABC was emphasized when Russ Rowntree, who was to acquire the Rosafe Farm when Astengo dispersed in 1958, sold a son of ABC. The price tag was an eye-popping $140,000, and the buyer was American Breeders Service, better known as ABS of Wisconsin. The ABC-bred celebrity was eulogized in speeches by the federal minister of industry, trade and commerce and the Ontario minister of agriculture and food. After a pampered journey to Wisconsin, the bull was suitably ensconced in Madison's leading hotel where he listened to speeches by such people as the governor of Wisconsin. And that's a lot of bull but it launched the youngster on a wave of publicity.

In retrospect, breeders who knew the ABC herd and have followed all its ramifications give Elgin credit for having an eye for good cow families and having the flair to promote the breed. There is also unanimity that it was a happy stroke that Hector Astengo purchased the ABC herd in its entirety.

While there is agreement on what Astengo achieved, there is confusion over what he was.

For Doug Dunton, "He was a bit of a loner. But he knew pedigrees and was very sharp in seeing what he could achieve by inbreeding ABC. There was far greater continuity when the Rosafe herd was sold than when Astengo acquired the ABC herd." Jack Fraser thinks, "It was fortunate that Astengo maintained the herd long enough to develop the cattle and maintain those bloodlines."

George Clemons recalls Astengo as "a greedy, selfish man. He could have been the most popular man in Canada but he ended by losing all his friends." In curious contrast, Jake, Bill McCaugherty's brother who spent a lifetime at *The Holstein-Friesian Journal*, remembers him as "a pleasant man; shrewd and very careful how he spent his money." "Shrewd" is an adjective also used by Elgin who adds, "If he told you he'd do anything, he would do it." Cliff Chant remembers him simply as "a perfect gentleman."

69

Johnnie Powell, who has directed extension for the Holstein-Friesian Association for many years, sums him up: "Astengo encouraged Canadians to return and compete in such major American shows as Chicago. He always collected, even though an animal which he'd sold might have gone bad; this is what marred his image in Canada."

But nothing seemed to mar the image of ABC. Seven years after his death, the legend was stronger than ever. The December 10, 1964 issue of *The Holstein-Friesian World* had a complete issue devoted to him. It was a fat publication with plenty of advertising, because so many breeders in Canada and the United States seized the opportunity to emphasize the involvement of ABC in their herds. The advertisements were in both English and Spanish, in recognition of the way the breed had penetrated Mexico and South America. *Sus mejores hijas son entre las grandes vacas de nuestra raza* ("His top daughters are among the great cows of the breed").

A feature article recognized the mosaic of ABC's breeding and that "His offspring are making history in many countries in addition to the United States and Canada." A photo feature was devoted to his daughters in the United States who had all produced more than seven hundred pounds of butterfat in a single lactation. Yet another feature traced the use of ABC descendants in the artificial insemination studs; practically every major breeding organization in North America had anywhere from one to six progeny of ABC. And so it went: a photo feature on the ABC sons which had been proved privately in United States herds; a review of his daughters and their remarkably high classification for type, and emphasis on their good udders.

Johnnie Powell, in a feature called "ABC Reflection Sovereign," observed, "Not only have his descendants come to dominate the show ring but they have topped practically every major sale in Canada during the past decade."

The history of dairy cattle breeding is marked with flamboyant meteorites which flame across the horizon and disappear as quickly. Modern cattle breeding is marked by the wealth of statistical data used to rate the true worth of animals. Gone are the days when a Holstein-Friesian bull could be promoted through the success of his progeny in a single herd, where environment could be a far more important factor than genetic worth. ABC had to compete in herds all across the North American continent. And then new lustre was added to the legend; he turned out to be a prepotent sire. His sons and grandsons began to achieve star status in their own right.

Just three years after *The Holstein-Friesian World* had produced what many had thought was the definitive ABC story, a second ABC issue was published. It was called "Reflections of ABC." The lead editorial noted that "Each generation of registered Holsteins seems to bring forth animals, both male and female, that capture the imagination of breeders. You are all aware of Holsteins that have accomplished this feat and ABC Reflection Sovereign is one of them . . . It is because of his proven ability as a sire and his almost universal acceptance by the Holstein fraternity that we have once again singled out ABC Reflection Sovereign descendants for special recognition."

Through the use of frozen semen, which had remained in storage for years after the death of ABC, some of his progeny turned up at recent sales. In 1971, Romandale had a reduction sale in which animals were paired in the auction ring; buyers had their choice and the other animal, in each case, was retained by Romandale. *The Holstein-Friesian Journal* reported that "A pair of young offspring of the great ABC and two of his 1961 daughters brought a total of $138,600 and all but a very few of the animals sold were rich in his blood." Symbolically, the aged dam of the sale leaders was knocked down to Rowntree Farms; she went to the farm which was once ABC and then Rosafe, and is now farmed by Russ and his son Tom.

One of the most intriguing sons of ABC was Rosafe Citation R. Citation R had a remarkable proof for both production and type of his off-spring. The wider a bull is used, the greater the likelihood of his proof declining. Not so with Citation R. In each succeeding year, both the type and milk production indices improved. But Citation R's progeny revealed that some of his genes were not those *de rigueur* with the Holstein-Friesian Association of Canada, he carried the "red factor." Some of his off-spring turned out to be not the traditional black and white but red and white! Citation R was sold to the Rancho Santa Monica in Mexico, where his ability to beget good-looking progeny which produced well was appreciated. The red colour is also appreciated in tropical countries because it gives the cattle greater heat tolerance. Ironically, Canadian breeders

71

belatedly recognized the merit of Citation R and spent a fortune in bringing his semen back to Canada from Mexico.

Jack Fraser says, "I would still rate ABC as the top bull . . . unless his son Citation R beats him."

Roy Snyder, who was the first lay-inseminator in Canadian AI and is now in charge of worldwide distribution of the semen of Canadian Holstein-Friesian bulls, says simply, "ABC Reflection Sovereign is the foundation of the modern breed."

Just as he had planned, Hector Astengo dispersed the Rosafe herd after ten years. The sale was dominated by sixty sons and daughters of ABC and twenty-two progeny of Inka Supreme Reflection who started it all when he bred Temple Farm May to produce the dam of ABC.

"Hector Astengo did exactly what he said he would do. Rosafe cattle mushroomed all over the world . . . and the greatest bloodlines go back to ABC," concludes Tom Hays.

Chapter 11

BLACK AND WHITE PERSPECTIVE

THE black and white cattle represent nearly ninety per cent of Canada's dairy herd. They have been exported to some fifty-one countries. In any one year, Canadian Holsteins, many tracing to ABC, may go to some twenty-six countries and earn some fifty million dollars in foreign exchange. The export of frozen Holstein bull semen is so large that it is estimated that this trade alone generates enough income to reduce by at least two dollars the cost of breeding a cow in Canada.

Japanese and Korean dairymen came to Canada to learn the ropes before returning home to manage herds of Canadian cattle. Canadian Holsteins have changed the national dairy herd in Spain, and the largest herd of Canadian Holsteins is in Italy. Go to Mexico's artificial insemination centre at Ajuchitlan and you'll find that thirty-eight of the forty Holstein bulls are Canadian.

Cuba has embarked on one of the world's largest attempts at genetic improvement in dairy cattle. The foundation is over twenty thousand Canadian Holsteins. The big impact is being made by the progeny of ABC. Move over to another Caribbean island, Puerto Rico, for a major black and white show and there is none other than Doug Dunton officiating as the judge; the whole show will have a Canadian atmosphere with Canadian bloodlines predominating.

Canadian Holsteins penetrated such iron curtain countries as Bulgaria and have even been exported to Holland, the home of the breed. Your world Holstein tour won't be complete without a visit to Italy's Cremona Show. Once again, it's really a Canadian show and the Grand Champion bull is a grandson of ABC. In Germany and Rhodesia, ABC progeny dominate both shows and production.

When it is Holstein Day at The Royal, you may find several hundred dairymen and traders in Holsteins, from Italy, France, Germany, Holland, Switzerland, England, Scotland, Ireland, Japan, Peru, Australia, Brazil, Mexico and many parts of the United States of America.

This is all part of the success story of Canadian agriculture; and no bull has had a bigger piece of the action than ABC. A show stopper is a great-granddaughter of ABC Inka May, Ingholm Rag Apple President, who broke the world's record for butterfat production.

Milk and butterfat production averages have now reached levels undreamed of just a generation ago. Prices have followed yields into the heady, rarefied atomosphere. Back in 1941, a herd dispersal average of $144 was described as "most successful." Recently, when a Pennsylvania dairyman sold an eight-month calf to Dr. R. D. Favera of Italy, he collected a cool $31,500. This was regarded as a realistic price, as the dam had produced well over 1,000 pounds of butterfat in a single lactation . . . and her sire was ABC.

Until 1972, the world record price for a dairy cow was held by Romandale Reflection Cristy, a granddaughter of ABC. When the Hanover Hills herd of Amenia, New York, was dispersed in November, 1972 all kinds of records were shattered.

Murton Shore of Glanworth, Ontario, put together a syndicate of Canadian dairymen which shot the biggest bankroll of all time for a single cow. It took $122,000 to buy the five-year-old Excellent cow, Tara Hills Pride Lucky Barb. That's $160 for every pound of hair, hide, bone and sinew! The Johns Lucky Barb family is rated so highly because of the impressive record of desirable type and excellent milk production . . . much of it attributed to ABC.

Each year the annual meeting of the Holstein-Friesian Association of Canada is marked with the recognition of Master Breeders. These are the

74

most prestigious awards given to the élite in the fiercely competitive business of breeding great cattle.

In 1974 ABC and his progeny brought this triumph to Alberta breeder George Oxtoby. Master Breeder Donald Budd had grade, or unregistered, cattle until 1954. It took twenty years of emphasizing the progeny of ABC to win the coveted Master Breeder Shield.

Master Breeder Fred Stewart attributes the incredible turn around in his herd to a daughter of none other than Inka Supreme Reflection and two of her sons. Of the thirty-nine animals which won the Master Breeder award for Stewart, there were twenty-four progeny of his foundation cow. Other prominent herd members were granddaughters of ABC. Albert ten Den emigrated from Holland to Canada and worked for several years at Rosafe Farms. In 1956, he picked up two animals at a local stockyard for a mere $116 and $99. Both were bred to ABC's son, Roeland Reflection Sovereign. Type classification of Very Good, milk yields of 25,000 pounds and a Master Breeder award followed.

When Richard Schleissner arrived in Canada in 1939 as a refugee from the Nazi invasion of Czechoslovakia he had just a single one-dollar bill in his pocket. He also had uncanny cow sense. He was one of the first to recognize the value of Roeland Reflection Sovereign who now has nearly five hundred daughters, with records of over one hundred thousand pounds of milk.

All Canadian AI studs rely heavily on ABC breeding. At the Western Ontario Breeders Incorporated at Woodstock, the headliner is an ABC grandson, Downalane Reflection Emperor, whose progeny excel in all three yardsticks—type classification, milk production and auction sale prices. Most of the WOBI bulls are grandsons of ABC and many also trace to ABC on the female side of their pedigrees. At the Eastern Breeders Incorporated at Kemptville, Ontario, another ABC grandson has been a perennial licence to print money; Seiling Rockman earned the Excellent accolade for type, as have twenty-five of his daughters and thirty-two of his sons. His daughters have prolific milk production and fifteen have topped the one-hundred-thousand-pound milk barrier. His nearly ten thousand classified daughters have rated sixty-two per cent Good Plus or Better.

Playwright George Bernard Shaw said it all long ago. His eye for the

75

ladies never dulled his repartee. When an actress burbled about the prospect of children with her looks and his brains, he countered with, "But what if they have my looks and your brains?" The remarkable thing with ABC is that so many of his progeny have his looks and the high levels of milk production of that great old brood cow, ABC Inka May.

The ABC Farms' Holstein-Friesian herd now comprises a single bull. Years after the ABC dispersal, Elgin got back into the Holstein business when he bought two bulls at auction, "to keep some of that good ABC blood." One proved to be a failure and was beefed, while Agro Acres Never Fear, who traces his pedigree on both sides to ABC, has now been favourably proven. The royalty cheques for Elgin's one-bull dairy herd keep trickling in; fast enough to show a profit for his second venture into the pedigree Holstein business.

Chapter 12

CRYSTAL LADY, QUEEN OF THE HIGH-STEPPERS

"THE night Mother retired Crystal Lady was quite a thrill; fifty per cent of the people attending the Royal Horse Show had tears running from their eyes," Elgin recalls.

The 1954 Royal had been opened in characteristic fashion by Field Marshal Viscount Montgomery of Alamein; when the fair closed eight days later it was on a different, nostalgic note, as thousands gave their last rousing cheer for the showiest, show hackney pony of them all.

The resonant tones of the master of ceremonies reverberated throughout the arena. "We pay tribute to a champion of champions in the harness pony world . . . Crystal Lady, owned and driven by Mrs. Elgin Armstrong of ABC Farms, has won fame at the Royal where she has won the Harness Pony Stakes in seven successive years. She has also brought fame to our country time and time again by winning harness pony stakes at Harrisburg, Pennsylvania, New York and Chicago . . . in 1948 Crystal Lady was judged world champion." You have to be very good to carry off the championship at Chicago's International Livestock Exposition.

The prancing Crystal Lady was driven triumphantly from the show ring for the last time. Then, the queen of the high-steppers was brought back into the arena where she was just about enveloped in a blanket of roses presented by Colonel Tom Kennedy. The band struck up "Auld Lang

Syne" and a remarkable pony, just thirteen hands in height, made her exit as befits a champion.

The hackneys have their origin in England and are now judged in two categories; the horses are 14.2 hands or more in height (a hand is four inches), the ponies have a maximum height of 14.2 hands. Hackneys are a reminder of more gracious times when beautifully costumed ladies drove their polished phaetons leisurely through the parks, rivalled only by their glistening, high-stepping hackneys. Whenever they paused for the courteous greetings of some dandy, the hackneys would assume a slightly spread-eagled stance. This is still a hallmark of the show ring hackneys and it has its origin in a practical consideration. Hackneys are very high-spirited and any change from that "parked" stance would alert the driver that they could be preparing to move off. And when they did, there was nothing to match the brilliant animation and rhythm of a perfectly trained pair.

The Carters have been farming in Chinguacousy for a long, long time. Jim Carter says, "I'll never forget how that yellow seed rolled out back in 1926 when Elgin threshed our clover. He was in a hurry but a good thresher. He was lean, but strong as a bull. The hackney horses were stronger then, too. They were bigger and stronger because they were worked a lot as a third horse on the farm and we'd harness up the hackneys when we drove to church." Canadian farm families, like the Carters, couldn't afford the luxury of a show horse. The hackneys had to be "legged up" with the stamina and condition to go all day, if necessary. While the modern hackney pony is less robust, it has an even more exaggerated gait. Every movement is precise and stylish. The ears and eyes are alert, and never more so than when the show ponies know intuitively that the judge's gaze is upon them. When the judge is looking the other way, the veterans of the show ring know how to relax. The best of the ponies peak when they "go down the rail," with each leg arching high and returning neatly and rhythmically, under the scrutiny of the judge whose life is hackney ponies.

As the postwar construction boom brought undreamed-of prosperity to the Armstrongs, Victoria was able to indulge in this expensive hobby, where even a clean sweep of the prize money just helps with the overhead. Crystal Lady was the first of the ABC show string and cost just $1,200; in her prime on the show circuit, bids of $50,000 failed to buy her.

Crystal Lady was like a delicate, finely tuned instrument. She was high-strung both in and out of the show ring. If she did make a mistake in the show ring, she tended to repeat that mistake in exactly the same place next time around the ring. Hard to catch in the paddock, she never failed to come up to greet Victoria Armstrong with a whinny.

It was Elgin who drove Crystal Lady to her first ribbon at the Oakville Fair. "And she was never beaten again, except by some bloody crook; and that wasn't very often." Some defeat of long ago must have still rankled, because only on rare occasions is Elgin heard to swear.

While Elgin is less than a dispassionate observer, the judging of hackneys is not a precise science. Veteran showmen believe that most times the best ponies win and they acknowledge that, just like people, horses have their days. But for people like Tory Gregg, who has been announcing shows for some forty years, "It is no longer a fun game and a family institution. It was fun, like playing professional hockey in my youth; now that too has become over-commercialized. It's all a matter of money and crabbing with the judges." Winning, with hackneys, is everything.

When I first saw Crystal Lady she was a venerable thirty-three years old. The lithe, youthful figure had gone and the back swayed down. But she still had that class, as she high-stepped across the lush bird's-foot trefoil pasture with its verdant leaves and brilliant yellow flowers.

Chap Carter, Jim Carter's brother, was the first of a series of trainer-managers to develop the ABC hackney ponies. He had a natural way with horses, developed from the days he helped around his father Matthew's livery stable in Brampton. Chap had the inevitable Armstrong apprentice-ship: he drove a gravel truck. Later he worked with the ABC Holsteins and then assumed responsibility for the hackneys, as they developed into the top show string in North America.

"Crystal Lady was a tough one, very high-spirited. It took me about a year before I finally got her going. I guess I was lucky. But right to the end of her show days you had to avoid doing anything which would rattle her and make her forget her good manners." Chap Carter had shown that he had a way with Crystal Lady. But, just before crucial judging at The Royal Chap, who was also an accomplished show jumper, broke a wrist in a jumping accident. "Crystal Lady wouldn't behave for any other driver, so Mrs.

79

Armstrong had Dr. Bert Bartlett of Brampton, a prominent hackney exhibitor and medical doctor, in attendance as I drove Crystal Lady.'' Chap, with a cast recently removed, had his wrist taped to give him enough strength to hold the reins.

The ABC show string expanded to include Golden Lady and Miss Adore; like Crystal Lady, they were daughters of King of the Plain. Then came Crystal Lady's offspring, Crystal King and Crystal Jewel. There were also King's Marvel, Christmas Eve, Pilot Model and Mr. Sandman. Cupid's Beau and King's Beau made a beautiful pair, each with their white blazes and white-stockinged feet.

ABC hackneys got more and more coverage in the glossy horse magazines. *Popular Horseman* of February, 1950 featured Crystal Lady on the cover of its annual hackney supplement: "Crystal Lady—Grand Champion hackney pony of both Canadian and United States competitions." The lead feature was on the ABC hackneys which were acknowledged to be always a threat, wherever they were shown. Just how much a threat they were, one realizes when browsing through the ABC tack room at Brampton.

Among the some ten thousand hackney ribbons, there are the most coveted from North America's prestigious hackney shows. There are also some fourth-place ribbons from some of Ontario's smallest country fairs. Some fairs were so small that the hackney judge was strong-armed out of the heavy horse ranks. The Armstrongs' rural roots showed up as they competed at such fairs as Ilderton, Elmira, Woodstock and Galt. Also in the tack room is the plaque of the National Equestrian Federation of Canada, which recognized Mrs. Elgin Armstrong as horsewoman of the year in 1964. There are enough coffee sets to stimulate an army and enough ornate silverware to overflow a jeweller's stockroom. There are silver cups and pots and urns and dishes and jugs, and a massive ebony block festooned with silverware: all in recognition of the winnings of Crystal Lady. There's a silver fondue set, and a huge silver punch bowl big enough to slake the thirst of a draughthorse. There are chafing dishes and vases and trays and entrée dishes, and combinations of glass and silver and wood and porcelain and sundry metals which testify to the imagination, if not the taste, of trophy designers.

Some of the trophies were won by the children of Elgin and Victoria Armstrong. Their interest in horses had been sparked from the day when eight-year-old Charlie returned home triumphantly with his Uncle Ted . . . and a Shetland pony named Playboy in the back of the car. The Brampton Horsemen's Association had their annual spring horse shows at ABC Farms. (There's veteran show announcer Tory Gregg at the microphone and secretary Charlie Armstrong checking the hackney entries in ring number one and the jumpers in ring number two.) The interest in hackneys was very much a family affair. Daughter Helen criss-crossed the United States and Canada with her mother showing hackneys. And her sisters Mary, Isabel and Ruth all enjoyed the occasional show. But sports page headings such as "Wife Shows Hubby in Winning Fair's Harness Pony Event" were more typical results of ABC entries into the competitive world of hackney ponies; you just don't capture major stakes events unless you go in there determined to win.

ABC ponies went first class all the way. Some trainers came from the United States and England. One trainer was so bitten with the importance of winning, that a lackadaisical ear, given to an occasional flop, might be wired in position. A glamorous beauty may owe much to the wiles of a cosmetician—but a horse with wired ears, a false tail and super-platform shoes also has more going for it than the gifts of nature.

The ABC ponies were always presented in the prime of health; even their teeth might have been suitably filed by veterinarians Glen Brown or John McKnight; their smallest nutritional wants were attended to. The harness and the phaetons were spotless, and at the major shows there was usually a plush little room beside the horse stalls for entertaining. Elgin took pride in his wife's accomplishments but showing hackneys was never really his bag; it didn't pay.

The industry of the entire Armstrong clan during those early postwar years was an incredible frenzy of successful livestock endeavour.

The brief fling with Holsteins was gradually being recognized as a watershed in dairy cattle breeding. Crystal Lady alone had won 555 of her 560 stakes events . . . and enough "hay" to pay for her oats. ABC Farms also had a string of successful jumpers, such as Black Velvet who was followed by Gray Velvet and Brown Velvet. Black Velvet, who was a winner

81

at such fiercely competitive shows as the Canadian National Exhibition, was sometimes ridden by Dick Day, who's son Jim holds a prominent place in Canada's Olympic jumping team. Together, they'd clear seven-foot barriers at Madison Square Gardens.

Leaf through those records of the early postwar years and you find the coveted diplomas of the Canadian National Exhibition, headed with the lines of John Milton: "Peace hath her victories/No less renowned than war." While the Velvet horses were jumping their way into the record books, ABC Inka May had copped the award of Grand Champion Holstein female, ABC Reflection Sovereign was crowned the Grand Champion bull and Crystal Lady had made a habit of walking away with the top hackney honours. Elgin was even showing his thoroughbreds.

No matter whether the stock was home-bred or purchased, exceptional individuals kept coming to the fore. Gray Velvet, who once traded as a gangling colt for just seventy-five dollars, consistently jumped high enough to become worth twenty thousand. The Armstrong luck seemed to be everywhere. Elgin bought Helicopter and promptly won the $123,000 Hambletonian, the first Canadian victory in this classic of United States standardbred racing. All that, plus construction in several provinces, was still not enough to absorb Elgin's restless energy. He tried his hand at the thoroughbreds, the racehorses of the sport of kings . . . with mixed success.

Chapter 13

THE SPORT OF KINGS

SOME institutions have a special Canadian flavour. Anyone who has enjoyed that rugged boat-race across the broken ice of the St. Lawrence River, knows that this is La Belle Province. Savour maple syrup from an Ontario bush and you know that this is the land of the Maple Leaf.

However, an Iowan driving through Ontario's Kent County and its sea of corn, developed by inspired plant breeders from the flinty maize of Indians, feels right at home.

Some institutions, like parliamentary government and fish and chips have migrated successfully from the United Kingdom. Watch a Bond Head sheep dog trial and you're back in England's Wiltshire. Swell the crowd at Toronto's Woodbine and . . . well, you may be unsure just where you are! You know that this is North America . . . but what's with the mediaeval dragoon of guards . . . and, yes, that is Her Majesty in the royal landau arriving for the Queen's Plate!

The Queen's Plate has been a Canadian, yet frightfully British institution, since 1883. The prizes include the Queen's fifty guineas and the most prestigious mantle in all Canadian thoroughbred racing: lure enough for Elgin, a recruit to thoroughbred racing circles.

It was an auspicious beginning. More Daisies, a mare purchased for just sixty dollars, foaled Armbro. In his first start, as a two-year-old at Woodbine, Armbro won in record time.

Given any luck, Armbro, Elgin's first home-bred horse, would have returned a handsome dividend for a one-dollar wager in the 1947 running of the Canadian Oaks. Like the first poll to report in a general election, Armbro just about summed up the Armstrong brothers' thoroughbred racing career. "Armbro forced the pace, held on resolutely when tiring, got to the front nearing the finish . . . but failed to hold the winner." Naming a filly simply, "Armbro," indicates that neither Elgin nor Ted envisaged that within a few years there would be hundreds of horses bearing the name as a prefix, and that it would be a familiar word on thousands of pieces of construction equipment.

Elgin was apparently something of a dark horse himself. Press reports of the time incorrectly identify him as "Jim Armstrong" and "A. E. Armstrong." In the coming years, just the name Elgin would be sufficient to identify the newcomer with an eye on the Queen's Plate.

The first Armstrong thoroughbreds were trained by Art Routcliffe who still maintains a successful public stable at the Ontario Jockey Club tracks. He soon had an Armstrong entry, Belflares, a two-year-old filly in the winners' circle at the now built-on Dufferin Park racetrack. Then, Heptad won the second division of the Clarendon Plate at Old Woodbine, now renamed Toronto's Greenwood. The prospects looked good; the *Daily Racing Form* headlined "Heptad Leads Juveniles at Woodbine." The handicappers rated the Armstrong brothers' Heptad and Trochanter, "Two of the top Canadian two-year-olds in training."

Trochanter came on strong, with the inimitable Eddy Arcaro in the saddle. A reporter noted that Arcaro "riding Trochanter, found his horse slowing up in the stretch and headed by Warren after leading most of the way. It looked like Warren's race but Arcaro didn't agree. He used his whip lightly, rallied his mount, found additional mileage and flew under the wire the winner. His ride was the talk of the track."

It looked like brothers Elgin and Ted Armstrong had arrived with a bang. However, a Toronto newspaper still felt it was necessary to open a 1954 Queen's Plate story with "The Armstrong brothers of Brampton, Ontario, are two unobtrusive gentlemen, neither of whom would be recognized by ninety-nine per cent of the patrons of Canadian racetracks." But neither of their two Bunty Lawless-sired colts, Trochanter and Heptad, was to win the coveted Queen's Plate.

Elgin, who had first been bitten with the racing bug with that old hollow-back-horse and who subsequently earned a living behind a team of Clydesdales, had set newer, higher sights. He planned to compete in England, the home of thoroughbred racing. He also wanted to buy some stallions of Hyperion and Nearco breeding. Nearco, when bred to the Hyperion mare Lady Angela, produced Neartic, the sire of the phenomenally successful E. P. Taylor sire, Northern Dancer, the most widely acclaimed thoroughbred ever foaled in Canada.

In July, 1955, the British sports pages noted that a Canadian buyer had topped the Newmarket sales with a bid of 5,100 guineas for Pipe Royal, a bay colt by Royal Charger out of Pipeclay. It was reported that Major P. J. C. Honner of Compton, Berkshire (a keen student of pedigrees who rated Nearco and Hyperion "Two of the greatest sires of all time") had purchased the colt for Canadian sportsman William Bovaird of Brampton. Bill Bovaird had actually been flown to England by Elgin to buy horses for the Armstrong brothers.

In the pioneer days of Peel County, Bill Bovaird's father, James, was a familiar figure as he peddled household necessities door-to-door. He acquired an ancient thoroughbred horse and not only speeded his deliveries but began what was to become a highly successful thoroughbred stable. Bill Bovaird was an ideal judge of horseflesh to scout the United Kingdom sales for Elgin. There have been thoroughbreds on the Bovaird farm for over a century.

The Bovaird name keeps popping up in the story of the Armstrongs. Typically, the Bovaird involvement is a mixture of thoroughbreds, gravel and construction. Bovaird, as Chinguacousy Township road superintendent and a member of Peel County Council, had sometimes locked horns with Elgin. "I remember one time when Elgin wanted to change a tender on gravel because of an error made by his bookkeeper. Elgin thought I was a little tough on him for making him prove that it was a genuine error. So I told him, 'As long as we understand that you are working for Elgin Armstrong and I am working for the ratepayers, we'll get along fine.'"

85

Unlike some strong-willed men, Elgin seems to have welcomed opposition for honing his own wits. And you had to be up early in the morning to outwit Bill Bovaird. His local nickname is "The Horse Thief"; the story is that he never travels without a halter. Having sold a horse and failed to receive payment, he spied the delinquent buyer coming down the road. Bovaird unharnessed his horse and left the hapless defaulter on the road with a pile of harness and an immobilized buggy.

Bovaird showed equal tenacity in putting together a string of United Kingdom horses for the Armstrong brothers. Transatlantic air flights and telephone calls had yet to acquire familiarity of use. When Bill Bovaird telephoned Brampton to report on his buying mission, "I was surprised that I wasn't talking with Elgin, but with my wife. It was a typical touch of Elgin's thoughtfulness that he had fetched my wife so that she would be the first one to talk to me in England."

Elgin flew to England with his old friends Wilfred Farr and Bill Willis. They had a great time. It was a new experience for the one-time Ontario farm boy to be poured into a rented morning coat and carefully creased trousers for a suitable entry into the Royal Enclosure at Ascot. "And to think even Ali Khan wasn't allowed in there," chortles Elgin. In Britain's society, even the prestige of the Aga Khan, a great patron of the sport, could not outweigh the strict taboo of divorce.

Other details caused Elgin some confusion. Used to a diet of Canadian cigars which never cost more than a dime, he was horrified to have to put down a fistful of British money which was still not enough to cover the cost of the hand-rolled Havanas which he encountered. Of greater relevance was the reaction to Elgin's racing colours which included gaudy, golden epaulettes decorated with two horseshoes. All eminently respectable on the North American scene but, as Major Honner gently pointed out, "That sort of thing just isn't done in England. You see, Mr. Armstrong, we feel that the horseshoes would have been unnecessary adornment."

Undeterred, Elgin had a ball in Britain, enjoying his first extended holiday from work in the better part of fifty years. The Canadian trio covered the United Kingdom in a rented plane, taking in the races at Newcastle, Ascot, Leicester and Sandown Park. At Newmarket, he bid 6,350 guineas to buy a couple of colts of Nearco breeding. It was a

86

memorable nineteen-day junket which saw the purchase of nine thorough-breds confirmed, some success on British turf and preparation for shipping the stallions back to Canada.

The grand finale came at Goodwood, with the exciting finish to the Sussex Stakes. The Queen watched and her colt Alexander appeared to snatch the victory from Elgin's My Kingdom. The Queen's colt was led into the winner's circle; but the judges had some reservations and called for a photograph of the photo-finish. The roles were reversed, the Canadian horse was awarded the victory and Elgin met the Queen for the first time.

Livestock Air Shippers Limited arranged a pioneer flight from England direct to Toronto. The cargo included the Armstrong horses, among them Running Water, winner of the Queen's Prize, and My Kingdom, fresh from Goodwood. But the transatlantic air shipment ran into trouble. The flight was grounded by bad weather in Iceland after the aircraft hit an air pocket and suddenly dropped a thousand feet or more and My Kingdom broke his halter and fell below Running Water.

Back home in Canada, the Armstrong brothers had some flat-racing successes. Double Life, a home-bred two-year-old, started as a 50-to-1 long shot and then "the youngster uncorked a burst of speed in the stretch which carried him to a length and a quarter win." Lord Elgin won at Wheeling Downs and Lady Ruth at Woodbine. The Routcliffe-trained horses, such as Admiral Armbro, romped home at Fort Erie, while Dominion Brave took the honours at Woodbine.

Subsequently, Art Warner trained the small band of Armstrong thoroughbreds which, in addition to Admiral Armbro, included Speedy Lament and Ouzo. "I enjoyed training for him for some three years and only wish I had met Elgin Armstrong earlier in my life. He's a gentleman and his word is his bond. The first spring I trained for him I was stabled at Woodbine. One Sunday morning he came out and watched several of the horses.

" 'Do you think you own these horses?'

" 'Mr. Armstrong, all the horses I train are handled as if I owned them.' "

Elgin considered this for a moment. "That's good enough for me. You have the green light to go ahead and do what you think is right."

87

"Only once in the next three years did he even telephone me about his horses. We developed Speedy Lament and Speedy Sonnet into stakes winners."

But, for all that, the thoroughbred venture was star-crossed. My Kingdom, who raced in Canada and California, was injured when he kicked the side out of a truck. In a single season there were three fatalities. Running Water died of a heart attack; an excellent prospect died from a bowel obstruction; a promising youngster, which had just been claimed for six thousand dollars, reared as he was being led by a groom, fell over backwards and died of a head injury. A foal fractured a shoulder; and so it went. Heptad threw his jockey before they reached the starting gate and raced a quarter of a mile on his own! The Armstrong luck seemed to have run out with the thoroughbreds. It might be the sport of kings, but it wasn't for Elgin.

"The thoroughbred is a kind of rattle-headed horse. I didn't really like the thoroughbreds. I couldn't see any way of making money with them. I had brought in some good stallions but we never did get good enough mares to breed them to.

"And that thoroughbred business, it's run by a clique. It attracts a different class of people than the standardbreds; it's all stockbrokers and bankers. Now the standardbred people! They are more rural and a better class to associate with."

Elgin "looked the situation over." He didn't see much prospect of emulating the tremendous accomplishments of E. P. Taylor in flat racing. To be a significant contender with the thoroughbreds would mean a large investment with little assurance of financial success. In contrast, the standardbreds were coming on strong right across North America. In Dr. Glen Brown, the Armstrong brothers had a farm manager who was steeped in harness racing. While the thoroughbred people were falling on harder times, the standardbreds were hitting a clip to make them one of the fastest-growing sports. By 1964, wagering on the trotters and pacers, the country cousins of horse racing, had outstripped thoroughbred betting by a wide margin and was never to look back.

Elgin had also become disenchanted with the thoroughbred fraternity's absorption with the odds and winning. "You'll not often hear a stan-

dardbred trainer talk about the odds of his horses. It's always performance. A good standardbred man with a top horse will say that he went
in one fifty-nine and three-fifths [a whisper under two minutes for the
mile]."

The once promising Armstrong brothers' thoroughbred stable was
down to a single horse. That lone survivor was "claimed" at Fort Erie,
when one of the Ontario Racing Commission's rules for acquiring another
man's horse was invoked. The claiming procedure stimulates competition
of equally rated entries. Elgin had no regrets. "There's more fun with the
standardbreds . . . You know, some of those poor fellas with the thoroughbreds haven't seen the light yet!"

But Elgin's foray into the world of the thoroughbreds had not been
without its pinnacles of pleasure. For a man who had known no elegance in
his youth and who even now has never been accused of sartorial splendour,
he had been won over by the colour, the pomp and pageantry of royalty.
But, even more, by the graciousness of Her Majesty Queen Elizabeth. He
was presented to the Queen on three occasions and also to the Queen
Mother.

In 1973 the Queen and Prince Philip returned to Canada for a serene
yet informal visit. It was June and time for the thoroughbred classic, the
running of the Queen's Plate. The loss of a contact lens threatened Elgin's
enjoyment of the day, while a shower momentarily drove the royal party to
shelter. But it was just a mixed-up rehearsal which preludes a great show.

Elgin was once again presented to Her Majesty, while Vivian was excited at the prospect of meeting royalty for the first time: "Elgin was tactful enough to refrain from reminding the Queen of that day at Goodwood
when he won in an exciting photo-finish."

Chapter 14

A NIGHT AT THE RACES

I didn't know a quinella from a quince or a trotter from a pacer. The marvels of a two-minute mile and a million other facets of standardbred, or harness racing, were yet to be revealed. I was a greenhorn at Greenwood, the Ontario Jockey Club track in Toronto.

It has been observed that one must spend either nine days or nine years in a country before becoming qualified to comment on any of the customs. Perhaps it's the same with the standardbreds. Ignorance and innocence provide their own unique vantage point. Nothing is accepted because that is the way it is done; one tends to question why and how such a complex sport works . . . or should one say business?

I boggled at the twenty-page official program; a blur of facts and figures in fine print. They say that if you don't know the players, you need a program. At the standardbred races, you always need a program.

The inside cover had a familiar name. The Armbro trainer, Joe 'Brien of Shafter, California, and late of Alberton, Prince Edward Island, was listed as an example, with the record of the mare Fresh Yankee so that any neophytes like myself could understand the niceties of the program.

On the opposite page, the Ontario Jockey Club Board of Trustees included one standardbred man amidst a sea of social-register names more familiar from thoroughbred, or flat racing; but Elgin Armstrong has always been a bit of a loner.

As I entered the clubhouse my eye was caught by large plaques which recall the outstanding feats of earlier years. Back in 1957, the Armstrong brothers had won with Captain Wright who raced the mile in two minutes and six seconds. By 1970, the pace had quickened and the Armstrongs' Horton Hanover, trained and driven by Joe O'Brien, had recorded the fastest time since 1936—1:59 and 3/5ths. There were other assorted accomplishments with horses owned variously by the Armstrong brothers or Elgin and Mrs. Victoria Armstrong and their son Charlie.

It was Thursday, February 17, 1972 and one of those crisp, clear nights which make the Ontario winter an enjoyable break between the colour of fall and the exuberance of spring. I probably saw the races that night as no one before or since. I had asked Ed Bradley, the Jockey Club's director of racing, to make it possible for me to see anything and everything. With such a carte blanche welcome, I saw much more than I had bargained for; I began to understand how the standardbreds attract and keep such a loyal following.

Interest surged, like electricity, through the crowd as the scarlet-coated marshal, astride a magnificent hunter, led the nine hopefuls onto the track for the first race. It was a mile to be raced at the pacing gait, as opposed to the trotting gait, and was open to maidens; this latter term, like so many others in standardbred parlance, has its own precise and peculiar meaning. A maiden has nothing to do with sex; it merely indicates that the race is open only to horses which have not won at this specified gait in any of their previous starts.

I watched from the vantage point of the mobile starting gate. The starting gate was patented by the late Stephen Phillips, whose invention is credited with raising the sport from the status of the country fair to its current, worldwide status at the major tracks on several continents. It was an innovation which put me front row centre for an exciting introduction to harness racing.

The starting gate at Greenwood is a gross Cadillac with welded pipe gates which can be extended on either side of the car like a pair of wings. Seated in a bubble above the roof, like an air gunner of World War II, was Ernie Brown, the starter. I have heard of back-seat drivers but I'd never before experienced the divided responsibility shared that night by starter

Ernie Brown and driver Bob Woodward. Bob steered the car but Ernie, facing aft in the bubble seat, controlled the throttle!

As we motored down the track, I noticed the "tote" board: the totalizer board which records all relevant details of pari-mutuel betting. The habitués could grasp at a glance all the many implications for the first race; but for a novice it was largely incomprehensible.

The parade marshal has done her job well in leading the horses out, five on one side and four on the other. They have turned and lined up behind the starting gate, with the number one horse in the post position on the inside of the track beside the rail.

The flashing tote board sign indicates that it is post time and, high above the grandstand, the race caller, Dan Loiselle, announces that "The horses are in control of the starter!"

Although Ernie Brown is directing the horses, everything is also scrutinized by the judges with an assist from a television camera. A lot of effort and many hopes have been invested in the race; everything must be not only according to Hoyle, but must also be seen to have been done correctly. As a further precaution, in the event of any subsequent controversy, movie cameras, located in the towers at either end of the stretch are filming the race.

Starter Brown's eyes are everywhere. He watches to see that each horse is at the proper gait and that there has been no interference. The starter is invested with authority to signal a recall if he is dissatisfied; a flashing red light would then alert both fans and drivers that the race preamble must be begun all over again.

The race judges, not only watch through their binoculars but they can also flip a switch and monitor an instant TV replay if they suspect any infractions. The begoggled and warmly clad drivers are on candid camera from the moment they drive onto the track.

But Ernie Brown is the man to watch and to listen to as he exhorts the drivers to get to the start on time. His voice crackles over the loudspeaker with a peremptory, "Get those horses turned around up there!"

The gate has been wound out and the horses are coming up behind us as we pick up a little speed. The horses are back perhaps six or seven lengths as we approach the starting pole doing some twenty-two mph and rapidly gaining speed. The back-seat driver keeps the gate just ahead of the horses. This is the moment that the horses have been bred for, selected for, trained for, and fed on a precise plane of nutrition enjoyed by few of the race crowd. To the uninitiated, looking fascinated through the rear window of the starting gate, a horrendous rear-end collision seems inevitable.

But Ernie and Bob are two more experts in a sport of expertise. Two horses are within inches of the gate, their nostrils flared and their breath condensing on the cold night air. And then we remorselessly climb away from the horses at some forty mph. The gates are wound alongside and we flee to the outer side of the track, leaving it clear for the pacers. I haven't a clue who could win, but root for the lone Armbro-bred horse, Armbro Kelly, who finished fifth, having led for the last three-quarters of the race only to lose at the wire. It was reassuring to find that the experts are not always that much wiser. The favourite, Etcetera, finished last in the field of nine horses.

The drivers go back to the paddock and watch their favourite program on TV: a rerun of the race. Meanwhile, the maintenance crews have their tractors warmed up and are on the track on the heels of the pacers. The track is groomed, once again, to its immaculate finish. The tractor drivers with their harrows have to keep a sharp eye out, as some of the horses in succeeding events race at full tilt, anti-clockwise around the track close to the rails; meanwhile, on the outer side of the track, horses with saddle cloths indicating their particular race, warm up at the more sedate trot, going in the opposite direction. To add to the apparent confusion, the "trot" in this instance can either be the trotting or the pacing gait. The fast horses are racing as if for real; the slower horses going in the concentric oval are really doing the equivalent of the human jog. Like finely trained athletes, the horses need warming up before the contest.

The second race is a trot. The trotter must maintain a gait which involves the diagonal legs moving in perfect harmony. In contrast, the pacing gait requires that legs on either side move in unison. Ernie observes, "I prefer to start the pacers. Except for the occasional free-legged pacer, all the pacers have hobbles, a set of harness which helps keep them on stride. The trotters are more or less freewheeling and there's nothing to restrict them and hold them on gait."

For the second race, Ernie has some excitable horses to contend with.

He knows what to expect because some have a shadow roll—a band across the nose which is designed to prevent shying at some shadow on the track. Another horse wears a red mask, rather like one of those grunt-and-groan artists of the wrestling arena. Still other horses may have a wad of cotton wool in their ears, or ear muffs. Ernie is more tense, and his responsibilities allow no room for small talk.

Gay Gillespie, the parade marshal, has left the track and the trotters are driven by such veteran horsemen as Keith Waples, Bill Wellwood and Ron Feagan mounted on their sulkies, or bikes. Ernie reacts to some comment from one of the three judges. These are the Presiding Judge, who is appointed by the Canadian Trotting Association, the Commission Judge, who represents the Ontario Racing Commission, and the Associate Judge, who represents the Ontario Jockey Club, the owner of Greenwood and other major Ontario tracks.

Ontario is gripped in frost and covered in a blanket of snow but here at the track we move off in a cloud of stone dust. With eight horses in line abreast, glued to the back of the starting gate, and the ninth horse behind them close to the rail, they are off to a perfect start.

We are promptly reminded that this is a hazardous sport. Driving high-spirited horses at thirty mph in a tight covey, each searching for racing room and each ready to take advantage of any opportunity, calls for nerves of steel and swift decisions.

Suddenly, the well-ordered scene erupts into chaos. The number seven horse has a foot caught in the wheel of the sulky drawn by horse number six. They stop abruptly and are promptly creamed by number eight, whose driver, Ron Feagan, lands on the track. This hardly slows his horse, Wheat Hauler, who departs driverless for the finish line. There is a chain-reaction accident, as Trader Midnite cannons into the wreckage and driver George Ferace is also dumped summarily onto the track.

Our souped-up Cadillac is first on the scene, and Bob leaps out with a wrench ready to remove the wheel which is trapping the hapless number seven horse, I.C.W. It all provides a revealing vignette of the spirit which pervades harness racing. Bill Wellwood, with unrestricted access to fifth-place money in the purse of $1,350, reined in Bonnie Speed to lend a hand in sorting out the melée. His prize money was automatically divided among the only four horses to finish the race. Harness racing is a blend of aggressive competition and camaraderie.

Back at the paddock, the victors and the vanquished all take the outcome of the disastrous second race with equal aplomb. There is no backbiting, there is no bellyaching; it's just one of the hazards of the game. Fortunately, none of the horses or drivers was hurt. In fact, Bill Megens, who drove Henry's Special, the unlucky number six horse in the second race, rebounded to win race number three. Starting from the unfavoured eighth position, Megens led all the way, outdistancing the field including the only other Armbro-bred horse of the evening, Armbro Jaunty.

My education continues in the paddock where I meet the Paddock Judge, Vince Polk, an ex-thoroughbred jockey who looks the part. His job calls for infinite tact, absolute integrity and inflexible firmness. Polk is responsible for seeing that every horse and driver is on schedule for the ten-race card of the evening. Then there is Dr. G. S. Elliott, the veterinarian hired by the Ontario Racing Commission. Says Elliott, "My duties include keeping any lame or sick horses off the track. If a horse raced well last week and then is allowed to race this week when he is lame, the bettors get pretty unhappy over the performance!"

The dapper Vince Polk seems to be everywhere, without appearing to hurry. He is watching to ensure that the horses are ready for each of the next three races. But horse number four in the next race, Duchess Riddell, has just thrown a shoe in her final warm up. Normally, an appointment with the blacksmith is more highly prized than one's appointment with the dentist. But here we are, one and a half minutes from post time on a Thursday night, and Duchess' appointment for next Tuesday is no longer relevant. Unconcerned, the resident blacksmith, Serge Bergeron, has replaced the shoe with graceful ease and ten seconds to spare.

My pass from Ed Bradley impresses a succession of security guards and I go by elevator up to the judges' eagle's nest, which is usually off-limits for everyone but the officials involved. Presiding Judge Alan McManus explains, "We have telephone communication with either end of the track, television and movie cameras following every move of the horses and a photo-finish camera located high above the finish line. We are also in contact with the various officials, such as the Paddock Judge, and we have a line to the mutuels. We also have instant replay on the television. Everything is double-checked before we make the official announcement of the placings."

William Lang, the Commission Judge, patiently points out that "There's a chart for every horse which records where they finished, their positions at the quarter, half and three-quarter poles and also the order in which they finished in recent races, together with the names of their competitors. If they are parked out—that is, forced to race for an extended period far from the rail, that too will be in the program. If they break their gait, that infraction will be recorded in the quarter during which it occurred."

I begin to get the feeling that this is an unusually regulated and honest sport. If a driver or a horse deviates substantially from the form or if there is a failure to race aggressively, then the driver is subject to penalties. Subsequently, I learned that John Bosworth, owner-trainer-driver, found that even his election to the board of the Jockey Club provided no amnesty when he broke the rules. He has been fined and disciplined just like any other driver.

I asked Judge McManus who was at fault in the pile up in the number two race. "It's just like driving a car, you've got to have your car under control at all times and it's the same with a horse race. The drivers are sharp and they have the quick reflexes which usually avoid the sort of rear-end collision we had tonight."

I remark on the efficiency of so many people, such as the blacksmith who shod a horse in one minute and twenty seconds. This occasions no wonder on the part of the judges and goes completely unnoticed by the thousands of fans packing the stands.

But we are now ready for the seventh race and I become aware of an erect gentleman of military bearing. He turns out to be Sergeant Reg Tucker of the Royal Canadian Mounted Police who has the power of life and death over the racetrack betting. He is in mufti tonight, since he represents Agriculture Canada. When he activates a shrill bell, the wickets of the pari-mutuel must close . . . instantly.

They're off! The three judges scan the field through binoculars, while the staccato voice of Dan Loiselle, the announcer, dominates the track.

"We're off and trotting . . . the inquiry sign has been posted. Do not destroy any mutuel tickets until the results have been declared official." Dan is the relief race caller and, at twenty years of age, the youngest in North America. But he has learnt fast. He gives the racing positions and the elapsed times at the quarter, half and three-quarter poles. He lucidly records the ebb and flow until, two minutes and ten seconds later, it's all over. All over, except to announce that the inquiry sign signified that the number one horse was off stride as it passed the fair start pole.

I descend to the ground floor of the massive clubhouse where I am welcomed by Bruce Kennedy, operations manager for the Canadian Totalisator Company which operates the betting machines and the computers at Greenwood.

"There are two computers which control the betting functions of the ticket machines, record the bets and then log them on magnetic tape. Each time the tote board cycles, you'll see new prices, new odds and the amount wagered for win, place and show," Kennedy explains. "The odds begin at the so-called morning line, which is the published odds in the program based on the record of each horse. Then, as the money is wagered, the odds change accordingly."

The electronic equipment would fill a fair-sized barn. It accomplishes all sorts of instant mathematical marvels. It computes the pay out on the daily-double, that is, what bettors win having selected the winners of the first two races. The exactor requires the exact order of the first- and second-place horses in given races, while the quinella demands the first two horses in any order. The wagering mechanism is operated by a staff of eleven using some five-million-dollars' worth of equipment.

There's a computer print-out on every race pool and copies go to the Jockey Club and the Ontario government to ensure that everything is above board. Government also has a degree of self-interest, as it skims its take from the bets and returns a percentage to encourage the breeding of racehorses.

Says Kennedy, "We guarantee the results. If our information on the wagering is inaccurate, then we are obligated to make up the difference." Finally, the tenth and last race has been run and Kennedy presses a

97

sequence of buttons. The computer is silent for the night and locked up until the information is retrieved the following morning.

For me, it has been a fascinating introduction to harness racing. But for thousands of others it was just a routine night, one of the thousands of race meets held every year at some two hundred tracks in North America.

Not everyone went away happy. One bettor lost his stake when his favourite transgressed by breaking into a gallop. He lost not only his stake but his temper, and was ultimately fined for smashing a plate glass window at the clubhouse! But his were not the only broken dreams. By 1 A.M. Greenwood was almost deserted. The floors were littered with torn and discarded tickets which had been purchased in euphoria for from two to fifty dollars. I reflected that it takes all sorts to make a race. There are the breeders, like Elgin, Ted and Charlie Armstrong who provide the underpinning which makes the sport possible; but they are only a part of this fast-growing sport.

There are all the owners, the owner-drivers, the trainers, the trainer-drivers and the "catch" drivers. There are the officials from numerous organizations and two levels of government. There's a supporting staff ranging from grooms to secretaries and purveyors of hot dogs and the gourmet chef up in the members lounge.

And then there's the cumulative effect of the bettors who, perhaps unwillingly, help finance the sport of harness racing. "They're silly, but God bless their silliness; we wouldn't have a job here without them!" says Kennedy.

I reflected on some of the diverse attitudes of the fans who have come to the track either to be entertained or enriched. The coldness of the night had done nothing to deter some of the bettors as they crammed the rail at the trackside for a closer view of the horses. For others, the horses came a poor second to the television screens, and they remained closeted in the fuggy warmth of the clubhouse. For them, harness racing is not breeding and training and racing; it's just winning and losing . . . probably most frequently the latter.

Each of the numerous TV screens located throughout the clubhouse has a convenient garbage container where the tidier bettors consign their shattered dreams with the tickets which no longer carry expectations of rewards. One bettor, totally absorbed by a TV screen, tossed his lighted cigar butt into a garbage container. The contents, mostly inflammable paper, burst into flames licking within a foot or two of the TV set. As the flames inched higher, no one moved to extinguish them. One hundred pairs of eyes were glued to the screen, and I began to get a feel for just how people react when they have their shirts riding on a race. As the heat increased, those in the front rows edged back without even glancing down. Their world was that little screen.

Tonight has been just another night at the races; tomorrow will bring new hopes and fresh horses.

Chapter 15

ARMBRO IN ORBIT

"I'VE just bought a mare that's going to win the Hambletonian. And when she wins the Hambletonian, I want you to paint her." said Elgin Armstrong to an astonished Betty Bell, who had made a reputation with her portraits of horses.

But buying a standardbred trotter that will win the Hambletonian is about as likely to succeed as building your own car to beat the pros in the Indianapolis 500 or throwing a saddle on the old grey mare for a runaway victory in the Grand National.

"I'd painted other Armstrong horses in the past, like Crystal Lady and Black Velvet. I don't care just to paint horses of wealthy people. I like to paint the honest horses. And there is honesty in horses, just like there is in people. But Elgin's claim to the Hambletonian was so outrageous I didn't even watch for the results," Mrs. Bell recalls.

The Hambletonian is named for one of the sport's foundation sires. Hambletonian was foaled on a New York farm in 1849, the most illustrious descendant of Messenger. Messenger was an English coaching horse which was brought to the United States in 1788. As the *Pennsylvania Packet* announced, "Just imported! The capital, strong, full-blooded English stallion Messenger to cover mares this season at Alexander Clay's, At The Sign Of The Black Horse in Market Street, Philadelphia. At the very low price of three guineas each mare and one dollar to the groom."

100

The pinnacle of the racing season comes in late summer with the travelling Grand Circuit series of prestigious races. An unusual feature of the Grand Circuit is the combination of large classy tracks and small country fairs. The Hambletonian is the three-year-old trotting crown of the Grand Circuit. In the early 1950s it was run at Goshen, New York, and is now housed at the Du Quoin Fair in Illinois.

"I was returning from a Florida vacation when I called in to see Del Miller training standardbreds at Orlando. I spotted a trotting filly I liked and asked Miller how much he'd sell her for," Elgin relates.

"$12,000," replied Miller.

"Well, he accepted my offer of $7,500 for her, plus the costs of training and whatever she won between my bid and his asking price in her first year of racing." As a two-year-old in 1952, Helicopter won $400.

Del Miller had trained three horses for the 1953 Hambletonian, which had attracted great interest because it was the richest running to that date; the total purse was $123,000. "I was down to drive behind Singing Sword and had Harry Harvey driving Helicopter. Before the race, Elgin wanted me to switch horses. But I told him I was committed to other owners long before he purchased Helicopter. We came as close to having words as we ever did. So I told him, 'You go up into the stands and watch the race and I'll run the stables!' " says Miller.

The first of three heats heightened Elgin's reservations. Del Miller stormed in second and Helicopter was a distant seventeen in a field of twenty-three, having broken at the start. In the second heat, it was an upset for the only filly in the race; Helicopter finished first by three-quarters of a length. She came back to win the third heat in even faster time. Harry Harvey, the youngest Hambletonian winner, made good Elgin's statement to Betty Bell. Elgin and Ted picked up the $64,000 first prize money, and the Hambletonian Cup left the United States for the first time in its long history. The filly, which had changed hands about as frequently as a dollar bill, had earned a permanent home and a place in standardbred history. A daughter of Hoot Mon, she was also the first offspring to emulate its sire's success in winning the Hambletonian.

Elgin, the extrovert and showman, had once again lived up to his reputation as "a long-headed old bugger." As with all his other sporting

101

and business ventures, standardbred racing was planned to show a profit. "We had to race and win the big stakes races to get records on our mares. Once we had established their reputation in the public's eyes, we could look forward to profitable prices for their offspring."

Just as Elgin had seen the potential in Helicopter, he found the potential in his soft-spoken neighbour, Harold McKinley. In a more exuberant moment, Elgin had called McKinley "the Del Miller of Canada."

"McKinley was a farm boy and good with horses. I'd watched him win with poor horses and figured what he could do if I gave him better horses to train." Elgin's faith was amply fulfilled as McKinley began building an Armbro reputation at the tracks. But having a few successful headliners was not Elgin's objective; he was one of the first to appreciate the sire Adios, whose daughters he coveted. Sometime army sergeant, Del Miller had spent much of his time in World War II in Burma and China furnishing horses and pack mules for the troops of Chiang Kai-shek. When he came back to the standardbreds, "I put up every cent I could find to buy Adios for $21,000." Adios made Miller a millionaire. Even by the time Adios died in 1965, his progeny had won over fifteen million dollars in prize money. Seventy of his offspring had clocked that magic two-minute mile and his last crop of foals fetched a cool seven million dollars.

"Gait is very important in a horse and Adios was the best balanced horse of them all. Once I'd got Adios going in the spring, I'd let out the hobbles three or four holes and he'd still be smooth and fast. That smooth gait is like the swing of golfer Sam Snead or that great baseball hitter Ted Williams. But Adios didn't just run smooth and easy; he passed on that gait to his progeny" says Miller.

Because of the restricted use of artificial insemination, the number of progeny which any standardbred sire leaves behind is strictly limited. Even for Adios there was a finite number of 550. "Elgin Armstrong saw the light years before anyone else in the States or Canada. He cornered the market, acquiring some forty Adios fillies to form a brood mare foundation second to none. He had the foresight to race them to get records and then retire them early. Some people would have chosen to race those good mares for ever. But he took the long view and now has daughters and granddaughters

102

of Adios," is the way Miller puts the Armbro breeding program into perspective.

Even now, the well over two hundred horses in the Armbro stables are
dominated by Adios' daughters, granddaughters and great-grand-
daughters, and the progeny of the most promising sons of Adios. By the
1970s, the United States *Trotting Association Register of Sires and Dams*
had grown to a fat volume of three thousand pages; analysis of the complex
statistical data on harness racing revealed Adios as the leading sire of
dams, based on the earnings of their foals. Elgin had backed his hunch in
going with Adios long before the data showed him to be such a dominantly
prepotent sire, who has done for the standardbreds what ABC did for the
Holsteins.

When Elgin was scouting the market for Adios fillies, there were
relative bargains to be had, when one considers that the Adios stud fee was
later to climb to $15,000. Dottie's Pick cost just $8,200 and went on to win
$264,000 before being retired to the brood mare band. Her laurels included
a world's record as a two-year-old and several miles in a sizzling 1:57 or
better. Dottie's Pick was the first pacing mare to top $100,000 in winnings
in a single season.

Dottie's Pick was so hot she was challenged to a mile "grudge" race
with another Adios offspring, Adios Harry, who had beaten the two-minute
mile on eight occasions and even shaved it to 1:55. Dottie's Pick had just
won the American Classic, worth $75,000, when she faced Adios Harry in a
$25,000-winner-take-all match at Yonkers, New York.

Three flights out of Malton Airport took the Brampton faithful to New
York to cheer on Dottie's Pick, the underdog. The home town press reported it as an exciting race and an outstanding victory for Dottie's Pick. But
trainer-driver Del Miller saw it rather differently. "I won by eleven lengths,
but it wasn't a good race. Dottie's Pick was in her prime but Adios Harry
just wasn't good that night; anybody could have beaten him. He had paced
hard all that year but he couldn't pace that night." Del Miller's disclaimer
to a famous victory epitomizes the best in this exciting sport. The trainer-
drivers remain remarkably modest and objective.

Another Adios daughter, Countess Adios, racing under the Armbro
colours is rated by Del Miller as "the perfect mare." As a free-legged

103

pacer, she won twenty-one of twenty-two starts one year, without wearing hobbles. She won major stakes races such as the Messenger and the Cane. Her winnings topped three hundred thousand dollars but she is best remembered for some rather unusual quirks. Prior to winning the Messenger Stakes, Del Miller warmed her up at the trotting gait. Then he went into the race at the pacing gait and Countess Adios performed perfectly, without the restriction of hobbles. Despite her excellent pedigree, her offspring were quite ordinary on the racetrack. However, the racing prowess skipped a generation and her granddaughters became champions.

Countess Adios had been originally purchased in partnership with Pennsylvania sportsman Hugh Grant; both Elgin and Grant were patrons of the Miller stable and both were determined to buy her! At the end of her racing career, Mr. Grant sold his half-interest and Countess Adios entered the brood mare ranks at Brampton. But not before she had racked up a remarkable achievement. The combined times for her best performances as a trotter and a pacer on a half-mile track were lower than any horse in history.

The Armbro trotters and pacers developed into a stable of stars. Sunnie Tar, a Tar Heel daughter, had a great racing career before being retired for breeding. She was developed by Joe O'Brien, the third and incumbent Armbro trainer. The Armstrong brothers bought Sunnie Tar on a bid of $7,500, primarily because she was out of the good dam, Sunbelle, by Mighty Sun. She earned a special niche in the Armbro stable with an unequalled record of nineteen miles in under two minutes. Her best record for the mile was a sparkling 1:56 4/5. Her lifetime winnings were a quarter of a million dollars.

A combination of concentrating on the daughters of Adios and mating them to the most promising studs soon gave the Armbro stable strength and depth. Nineteen Armstrong-bred or -owned horses have won over one hundred thousand dollars each for a total take of some four million dollars. Farm manager Dr. Glen Brown points out that "37½ per cent of the world championship records restricted to fillies and mares were held at one time by Armstrong-owned mares. This domination of the record books has earned our brood mare band a reputation as being the best young group of mares owned by any farm."

104

Some of the sires used by the Armstrongs are home-bred; like Armbro Express, a fleet son of Adios and a winner of the Canadian Cup and the Canadian Standardbred Futurity. Then there are the syndicated stallions; the Armstrongs have a number of services to each stud in proportion to their share of the syndicate. The top sires include Nevele Pride, Bye Bye Byrd, Most Happy Fella and Hickory Pride, all with track records well under two minutes.

One system of picking winners at the racetrack is to go for the funny names; sometimes it is quite as effective as the most experienced handi-capper's techniques. But there is no fun in trying to generate original names for scores of colts and fillies every year. Glen Brown's system is to begin the name with the Armbro prefix and then follow with a name starting with a letter which denotes the year of birth. But the system is even more complex than that. With the emphasis on brood mares, there is also an effort to have names which are readily identified with families.

Helicopter was the mare which put the Armbro stable into orbit and her progeny are all named with an airborne connotation. Her fourth foal, sired by Star's Pride, was aptly named Armbro Flight. She turned out to be the fastest thing on four legs in North America. As a three-year-old trotter, she beat the two-minute mark. In her brief racing career of just three seasons she won $493,602 in prize money.

Probably no horse in the history of the sport in Canada has gained such a warm and wide following. Her track achievements earned her the Canadian Trotting Association Canadian Horse of the Year Award for an unprecedented three years in a row. Her last race was one of her out-standing triumphs. Despite a sore tendon, she came from behind to win by a length in the $100,000 Roosevelt International Trot. This is a demanding mile-and-a-quarter race, which took Flight just 2:31 3/5; a record for the event. Joe O'Brien likes to finish strongly and that race was no exception; they came home doing the last half-mile in just 59.4 seconds, bringing the crowd to its feet in a standing ovation.

"She's the greatest horse raised in a hundred years as far as I'm con-cerned," declared Elgin. And his claim has not been disputed. Only one prize was to elude Flight. Just thirteen years after Helicopter had put the Armstrong brothers on the map, Flight took a crack at the Hambletonian.

Like her dam, she was the only filly in the field, but the best she could do was to win one of the three heats.

Now Flight has also joined that illustrious group of brood mares at Brampton. Her foals Orbit and Pageant are among the third generation of that airborne dynasty, which is promising but unproven. Flight's full brother, Armbro Jet, after a very successful racing career, now stands at stud with such other Armbro faithfuls as Horton Hanover and Armbro Express. Elgin sure started something when he spied that little filly in Del Miller's stable and bought her to win the toughest trotting contest in North America.

The 1973 North American results show the stature earned by the Armbro stable. With winnings of over one and a half million dollars, Armbro ranked behind the celebrated stables of Hanover, Castleton and Almahurst. In the contest for purses won by two- and three-year-olds, Armbro moved up to third spot. But, in the all-important category of average earnings by two- and three-year-olds, the Armbro stable, with $13,852, came in first place in North America.

H. G. Strong

(Upper) The third heat of the prestigious Hambletonian at the Du Quoin, Illinois State Fair gets away to a brisk trot behind the starting gate. *(Lower)* Harry Harvey teamed the Armstrong brothers' mare Helicopter to an upset victory in the 1953 running of the Hambletonian.

Edward McGarty

Helicopter's speed brought the coveted Hambletonian Cup to Canada for the first time; Elgin in his usual direct fashion set out to win the Hambletonian . . . and did.

Karl Hubenthal

Dottie's Pick, a star of the Armstrong stable, is just one of the outstanding daughters of Adios who make up the brood mare band.

E. L. Boutilier

Del Miller (right) owner of Adios and Meadowlands Farms in Pennsylvania, trained and drove numerous Armbro horses to victory before handing over the reins to Joe O'Brien.

United States Trotting Association

Made for each other; Armbro Flight, a Star's Pride daughter out of Helicopter, with Joe O'Brien in the sulky as they narrowly defeat the French trotter Roquepine in the 1966 running of the Roosevelt International.

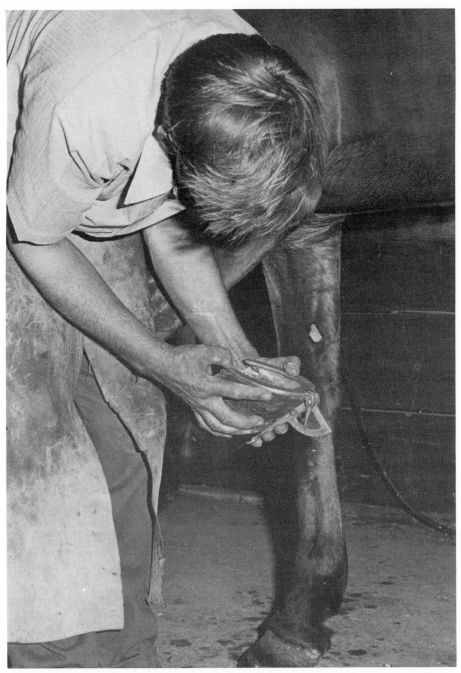

Peter Lewington

Blacksmith Ed Vincent of Woodbridge, Ontario, checks the precise angle and length of toe of Armbro Noranda; he also put the first set of shoes on Armbro Flight, sending her on her way to winning nearly half a million dollars.

Michael Burns

Armbro Indigo (left) in a carefree, playful mood also took racing seriously and set a track record at London's Western Fair Raceway.

Armbro Flight shows the speed and style which made her the darling of race fans across North America. Joe O'Brien in the sulky is the 'ice man', noted for his cool technique of coming from behind for a strong finish.

Charlie Armstrong discusses the intricacies of standardbred pedigrees with (right) Duncan MacDonald, owner of such stars as Fresh Yankee and Armbro Nesbit.

Bill Bovaird (left) flew to England for Elgin to select the foundation of the Armstrong thoroughbred stable.

Armbro Express, a son of Adios who has himself broken that magic two-minute mile, now stands at stud at the ABC Farms at Brampton, Ontario.

Elgin.

The camera confirms a victory for another great Adios daughter, Countess Adios.

This is the peaceful Ontario countryside where the ABC legend was born.

The last of a long line of ABC hackney ponies is driven by Helen (Armstrong) Southgate . . . while the trainer clutches the final ribbon.

Gordon Campbell

A corner of the Brampton yard; the rest of the construction fleet could be scattered between Edmonton in the West, Thunder

The orange Peel equipment became a familiar sight in several provinces.

R. A. Lowndes

Arrival of an asphalt plant alerted Ted Armstrong to dream up innovations which resulted in output exceeding manufacturer's specifications.

Brampton Daily Times and Conservator

Brampton Daily Times and Conservator

Armstrong Brothers

Peter Lewington

(Top left) When the Etobicoke burst its banks, mini-icebergs and flood waters swirled down Brampton's main street. *(Top right)* The fishing was allegedly good down on Main Street. *(Bottom left)* In the early 1950s the Armstrongs built the Etobicoke River flood control channel. *(Bottom right)* . . . just in time to divert the deluge of Hurricane Hazel.

Even well-bred pacers like to kick their heels up once in a while.

Chapter 16

NO TWO-MINUTE MILE COMES EASY

The "jugheads," as the flat-racing fraternity disparagingly calls the standardbreds, took up to three minutes to pace or trot a mile in the early days of the sport. Joe O'Brien has shaved that time to an incredible 1:52. But despite that wing-footed progress, a two-minute mile is never taken for granted. It's that something special in harness racing which brings any crowd to its feet; they know that no two-minute mile comes easy.

Glen Brown has had a hand in developing over twenty Armbro horses which have broken that speed barrier. When Glen came to manage ABC Farms in 1958, he was no stranger to harness racing. His father, Jim, had been a horse dealer in northern Ontario and was subsequently very active in the Canadian Trotting Association, the Canadian Standardbred Horse Society, and was the only man ever to win the Canadian Pacing Derby on four occasions.

When Dr. Brown came to Brampton, having graduated from the Ontario Veterinary College, he became responsible for a small racing string of a dozen mares trained by Del Miller, plus another eighteen with trainer Harold McKinley and a crop of four yearlings at the farm.

"We began acquiring and retaining fillies of the bloodlines which we thought would make them desirable as brood mares. But first, we had to determine their ability and the only way to do that is on the racetrack. Ours

107

is a breeding operation with emphasis on the lower side of the pedigree. You can't buy, at a single stroke, a good brood mare band. You have to build one steadily on conformation and soundness and the results of the races," Brown says.

"We have a different approach for the male side of the pedigree because the public only wants colts by the ultimate horse, the champion, the really great one. No single farm is ever likely to breed enough sires of that calibre to sustain a breeding operation. There are very few horses which achieve that level, and you destroy prices in your own yearling sales if you retain all your best colts."

Nor can you buy all the sires you need; even in a sport where bankrolls of several million dollars are flashed around, no one has that kind of money. So Armbro hedges its bets. There are the home-bred and wholly owned studs like Armbro Jet and Armbro Express. Also standing at Brampton is the phenomenal Horton Hanover whose track records have acted like a magnet, drawing some of the best North American mares to his harem; even in his first breeding season, he bred over 130 mares. Then there are those prestigious, syndicated stallions; Armbro will have a piece of the action, perhaps five services to a stud horse which may be used or sold in any season. Enter yet another category of super-sires. "In addition to seventeen syndicated stallions, we patronize other sires. This is a practice which gives us access to such standouts as Meadow Skipper and Bret Hanover. We don't own a share of such horses but we book services for some of our best mares. This is where the value of a good brood mare band shows up. No one with a great stallion will accept anything less than a high-quality mare which holds promise of enhancing the sire's reputation when his colts go to the races; if you just have a nickel mare, they'll say 'Sorry! We haven't any room.' "

But who do you breed to what, and why? This is a crucial decision in the pursuit of a two-minute mile. Dr. Brown is a big man in a big job but he doesn't make these decisions alone. Elgin is involved because he has that intuitive instinct of a breeder. Brown says, "We go over the options with Joe O'Brien because his opinion is also extremely valuable. He has raced a lot of these mares and he knows their habits and their gaits. He has either raced the sires or raced against them.

108

"We then make a list of the mares which are in foal, in chronological order of foaling. Because the first rebreeding is done nine days after foaling, we have to ship the mares in foal to the farm wherever the particular stallion is standing. And as many of the sires are in the United States, that's where most of our foals are born. Around November, we develop a second list of the barrens and maidens, to determine their heat cycles. We want to breed them so that they foal shortly after November 15 of the following year; for record purposes, any foal dropped in November or December does not have his first official birthday until one year from the following January 1. This gives them a little extra age and size when they first go to the races as two-year-olds."

The form-filling that has to be done would make the paperwork needed for Henry Kissinger to complete a state visit to Cuba look like a mere scratch pad.

First, there is the health status. Staff veterinarian John McKnight, who incidentally has a fast-trotting mare of his own stabled out at Orangeville, Ontario, says, "Sometimes, I find it hard to believe that I get paid for going to work because I enjoy it so much. My job is disease prevention. Even with over three hundred horses, there are lots of days I don't have to treat any of them for sickness or injury." Dr. Brown's secretary, Shirley Butler, maintains the health charts for each horse; she records that the various vaccinations have been done on schedule and that the insurance policies are up-to-date. There is also a raft of custom and export papers to be completed. Finally, with computer efficiency, the actual shipping schedule has to be made up so that each female reaches her prearranged beau.

"Most of the shipping is done in our own thirteen- or nine-stall horse vans. You see, I was born on Friday the 13th and so I'm not superstitious like some of them over in the construction end of this business!" laughs Dr. Brown. "Most of the mares have been shipped so many times they don't present any problems. There's the odd exception, like one who's a nightmare to ship because she'll always try to lie down while we are loading her."

It all begins to look like the old chicken-and-egg story. You have mares because your business is selling their offspring. But you can't sell the offspring at a profit without good race times. So even before the foals are born, Glen Brown will be ruminating on the stakes and futurity guide of the United States Trotting Association. Nominations and payments in a futurity have to be made prior to birth and the sustaining payments have to be made at intervals right up to just before a big race. On the offchance that he may have a contender for, say, the Messenger Stakes, Dr. Brown may begin payments for perhaps forty foals in this pacing event. Similarly, the most promising from the trotting families will be entered for the Hambletonian. "The wastage is tremendous. For some of the major stakes events, the original nominees could number thousands. By the time a race is run, that list may be whittled down to just a handful of horses. But all those payments have contributed to the sort of purses which can make racing profitable," says Dr. Brown.

Once a mare is pronounced safely in foal, the whole complex business of charts and papers and van schedules begins all over again. For most of the gestation period, the mares will remain in the Armbro fields and barns in Peel County. A month before they are due to foal, they will return to the United States for the next phase of the cycle. Birth is always an anxious time; Bonjour Hanover, a full sister of the great Bret Hanover, was purchased for $75,000 to fill a special niche in the brood mare band—only to die with her first colt in a difficult foaling. A live foal is defined as one that stands alone and nurses. Having accomplished that feat, the bills become due for the stud fee which is in addition to the groom and stabling costs.

Then it's back to Brampton again. That first summer is idyllic for the foals. They gambol with their dams in the lush fields, which are fenced to avoid any forseeable hazards. The colts' carefree existence continues until the latter part of their second summer, at which time they are prepared for the yearling sales. But there's nothing carefree about the costs. Operating a breeding farm is expensive. It can cost some eight thousand dollars to bring a yearling to a salable age.

Next comes the training, which calls for infinite patience and skill. First, the yearlings are "ground broken." A yearling must get used to the bridle and then have a girth tightened around him. One man will walk behind, driving him, while two men with lead shanks walk on either side. Once a colt is accustomed to these minimal restrictions, he is hitched up to a training cart. Again, for the first few outings there will be men on either side with those restraining lead shanks. Later, one of the lead men is taken

110

off and finally, when the trainer is sure that the colt is ready, he will be driven from the sulky.

Jack Kopas, who maintains a public stable at the Western Fair in London, Ontario, usually has several of the yearlings owned by Ted or Elgin or other members of the Armstrong family.

A public stable is one operated by a trainer who is an independent contractor for horses from a number of owners. This is in contrast to a private stable in which the trainer operates under contract to a single owner. Operators of a public stable bill clients for all expenses, collect an agreed fee and have the added incentive of retaining ten per cent of any winnings.

Jack's forte is developing colts. By 5 A.M. the night watchman has been joined by the staff of grooms. There'll be a feed of oats, and by 6 A.M. the boys (grooms) will be out lightly jogging the horses round the half-mile track. Back in the stable, each is cooled with a woollen blanket and given a couple of flakes of choice baled hay. The timetable for feeding and watering is strictly adhered to. There will be a different feeding regime for the colts in training and for those which are ready for the races.

Jack Kopas draws up an individual training schedule for each colt. This may mean a couple of miles of jogging, followed by a mile of working in some three minutes. Following a rest of half an hour or so, the colt may be back on the track to do a mile in 2:45 to 2:50. Exactly. Trainers, like Jack Kopas, carry a stopwatch cupped in one hand so that they can check the times at each quarter. "I like to train my horses in groups of four so that they become used to competition. If you don't train a horse this way you can find that when he gets into a race he just isn't ready."

Most of the Armbro neophytes will be pacers. Dr. Brown says, "A trotter races free of restricting hobbles and tends to break his gait more frequently than a pacer. Consequently, the public is less inclined to wager on the trotters. There may be one or two trots on a race card and the rest will be pacing events." For Elgin, there's nothing to match "the beautiful gait of a pacer. When you get a really good pacer, you can set a glass of water on his back and he can pace without spilling it!"

Each fall, the most promising Armbro fillies and some of the purchases from the fall sales are flown out to Shafter, California, to be trained by Maritimer Joe O'Brien.

Prince Edward Island is known as the cradle of Canada's Confederation. It is also the home of harness racing and the birthplace of Joe O'Brien. "My dad had a training track on our fifty-acre farm at Alberton and I helped him since I was old enough to carry a bucket of water." One of Joe's first "big" wins came at Port Elgin, New Brunswick, during the depression. "I had a green horse then and he did much better than I had expected in the free-for-all. I won twelve dollars."

Since then Joe O'Brien has been first to the wire over three thousand times. He has clocked more two-minute miles than any other driver in the history of the sport. His winnings have long since passed the ten-million-dollar mark. Elgin affectionately calls him "a banty rooster who is worth two seconds with any horse."

Joe O'Brien has the lightness and grace of a jockey and very nearly was one. "I even had an offer to ride for a large New York stable, but I love the harness horses and I would not have been happy doing anything else."

He began building a postwar reputation as a trainer in the United States and was sent by his California owners to an eastern sale to buy that great son of Adios, Bret Hanover. Then, the night before the sale, he recieved word that his owners were selling out. He was unemployed. But not for long. Del Miller had reached the point where he could not handle the rapidly growing Armbro stable. He promptly, and with characteristic generosity, persuaded Elgin to let Joe O'Brien train some of the horses. Not just any horses, but such promising prospects as Armbro Flight. O'Brien proved equal to the challenge and has never looked back.

The rapport which has developed between Elgin and Joe is probably only rivalled by Joe's uncanny affinity with standardbred horses. Joe will squat in a field and quietly talk to the horses until, one by one, they come up to him. Even usually rather unsociable mares, like Armbro Flight.

Glen Brown comments, "Joe knows how to discipline a horse without ever using a whip. Watch him in a race, and you may think that he is using the whip on his horse. But all he does is bang on the shafts or the back pads. He just rattles around to get the horse's attention."

Part of that unique bond between Elgin and Joe has been forged from

112

O'Brien's habit of finishing with a "lot of horse." He knows that there is a fine line between getting the best out of a horse and breaking his heart by overtaxing him. Elgin says, "So many drivers get too anxious. Joe is the ice-man. He just sits there and freezes. He may be lying fourth or fifth coming into the home stretch. But so many times, he has enough strength saved in his horse to come from behind. He has won more races that way than any other driver in the world."

The technique varies with each race and each horse; O'Brien just seems to know what is needed to get the best out of a horse. For the Ken-tucky Futurity, Joe felt that Governor Armbro needed the unusual warm-up of a brisk gallop before the race, having just freed a locked stifle joint. Despite a little soreness in his feet, Governor Armbro trotted first under the wire—and within ten yards had broken. Had he broken earlier, it would have cost a purse of thirty thousand dollars.

"I've never known anyone like Elgin," says O'Brien. "Even though he is seventy-six years old, he looks ahead as though he were twenty. Having proven a filly at the races, he's content to return her to the farm as a brood mare. He has never interfered with any decision I have made and he is one owner who can enjoy a race even though he doesn't win. I can tell when he is pleased, but he is not the kind that wants a big celebration on a win and has a long face when he loses. Some owners want to celebrate with cham-pagne and when they lose they look like somebody's died.

"I think that many people would be surprised if they knew how much psychology there is in a horse race. If you get a filly tired and weak near the end of the race, she'll get discouraged and may get into the habit of losing. I like my horse to feel she's beating somebody, even when she isn't. Sup-posing there are three horses in the race that I know I can't beat, regardless of what I do. My horse feels a little brighter at the finish when she passes some horses to finish in fourth place. But if I'd gone to the front and then been beaten by three horses, she wouldn't be as confident at the next start."

Hit a long, hot streak, as Joe O'Brien has, and you'll spend more time in an aircraft than a sulky. Joe may race at Windsor, Ontario, and then fly on to Garden City, Ontario, for a second meet and even complete the day's activities with a race at Buffalo, New York. "It can be done, but it does take a little preparation," says Joe with fine understatement.

113

Joe O'Brien is one of that select group of trainers who have done so much to enhance the integrity and quality of harness racing. Despite all the big purses and fast times, he still cares about horses: "Like some of those poor old horses in the claiming races where they're patched up week to week just enough to get by. It's pitiful to see some of them so sore they can hardly walk back to the barn. They should be retired and turned out to pasture."

Joe O'Brien added to his racing laurels with Armbro Flight, a horse he regards as one of the gamest he has ever trained. But his biggest money-spinner was Fresh Yankee, owned by former sawmill operator, Duncan MacDonald, of Cape Breton Island. MacDonald picked up Fresh Yankee at a Harrisburg sale on a bid of nine hundred dollars, apparently in ignorance that eight hundred dollars had been spent on vain attempts to cure colitis.

Joe O'Brien was just what Fresh Yankee needed. He took her to the front to win purses of $1,251,502 until, as a tiring nine-year-old, she was second to Speedy Crown in the 1972 Roosevelt International.

In one of the most graceless moves in all standardbred racing, Mac-Donald not only took Fresh Yankee away from Joe but inferred that he hadn't even tried. Taking over the reins, MacDonald backed his own judgment and finished fourteen lengths back in a rematch with Speedy Crown. MacDonald reluctantly accepted the inevitable; Fresh Yankee had earned honourable retirement. She was placed in the care of Glen Brown, along with the other brood mares at Brampton.

An outraged O'Brien refused to drive Armbro Nesbit, another star in the tiny MacDonald stable. Finally, a whole year of Elgin's quiet and tactful diplomacy resulted in a reconciliation, and O'Brien resumed the training of Armbro Nesbit. The style of the two drivers could not be more different. MacDonald drives to win, every time. O'Brien drives to win, bearing in mind the condition of his horse. Joe and Nesbit carried on an impressive string of victories worth $340,000, only to be beaten, ironically, by one of the few horses which O'Brien had ever given up on prematurely—Invincible Shadow. Having paid sixteen thousand dollars for him O'Brien sold Invincible Shadow for just five thousand, only to be later defeated by him in the American Pacing Classic at Hollywood Park in

114

California. But then no race, and certainly no two-minute mile, ever comes easy.

Joe O'Brien is nothing if not resilient. Nesbit enjoyed a winter's rest and came back in peak form to show Invincible Shadow a clean pair of heels in a decisive victory in the fifty-thousand-dollar running of the Provincial Cup. For Joe O'Brien it was not just another two-minute mile . . . it tasted sweeter than most. It was also the tonic needed by Joe and this great son of Bye Bye Byrd to set a new record. This time it was the Old Glory Pace at Yonkers, New York. They came out of the number one position . . . and stayed in front to win in a sparkling 1:56 4/5. It was a new night time, half-mile track record, surpassed only by Albatross and Strike-out in daytime racing. The best times are usually set on the still, hot and humid days of summer—not on cool evenings.

Chapter 17

GO RALPHY BABY!

N ADIR, the dictionary states, is the opposite of zenith: the lowest point, as in "the nadir of our hopes." Dr. Don Davis, owner of Armbro Nadir, knows differently. So do the pacing fans, from Montreal's Blue Bonnets to Winnipeg's Assiniboia Downs and Edmonton's Northland Park. For them he is "Ralphy Baby" and the fastest pacer ever bred in Canada. His name rhymes with that of consumer critic Ralph Nader, and that's enough to coin a catchy nickname.

For nineteen years, Don Davis had been a veterinarian in practice at Uxbridge, Ontario. Then, a few years ago, he moved to Guelph to become cattle diseases consultant to the Ontario government. Still not quite a nine-to-five job, but one which gave him time for a hobby. His standardbred venture began cautiously with a one-quarter interest in Norwen Express, an Armbro Express colt. "A good, honest racing horse. Then I wanted a good raceway horse to compete at tracks like Elmira and Mohawk."

The 1972 Armbro yearling sale had been the most successful ever. In contrast, disease, in the form of virus enteritis, had struck one isolated barn, marring the preceding year's sale. Twelve colts had died and twenty were too stunted to go to the prestige fall sales. Once the disease outbreak had been curbed and the colts pronounced fit, Glen Brown decided to market them privately as partly trained two-year-olds. The remnants of the 1971 crop were finally sold in 1972.

"Armbro had the sort of mares I like and Airliner was the type of stallion that had caught my eye," Davis says. "I made notes on the three colts I liked best. Then I got Glen Brown and John McKnight to do the same. 'Ralph' was on the top of my list and he was the only colt which appeared on all three lists. He was a big, healthy colt by then. You have to give Armbro credit for the way they put the bone in their colts. They accepted my offer of $4,750 and then I tried to sell three-quarters to my partners in Norwen Express. They all said no, and they've been regretting it ever since!

"I'd liked the way Nelson White of Rockwood, Ontario, had trained Norwen Express. 'Whitey' had always been straightforward with me, very honest and above-board, and he always brought me back a good horse. He became Ralph's trainer.

"By the fall of 1972, Ralphy qualified at Mohawk. He broke in his first race but went on to win in a startling burst of speed. This was the first time we felt we had anything other than a very ordinary raceway horse. He won his next two starts and then we laid him off for the winter because he picked up an influenza virus. By March he was racing at Greenwood and won six starts."

Ralph Baby, moving in more exalted society, went to Montreal's magnificent Blue Bonnets track, which held the record for the fastest times in Canada. They had been set on the trotting gait by Nevele Pride at 1:59 3/5ths and by Romulus Hanover on the pace at 1:57 and 1/5th.

At Blue Bonnets, White teamed Ralph to their first two-minute mile and, as usual, never touched him with a whip. A few weeks later they were back at Blue Bonnets for the $130,000 Prix d'Été, the summer pride of La Belle Province. Whitey and Ralphy started from the unfavourable number seven position in a field of eight, and the bettors gave them just a thirteen to one chance of winning. With White rocking in the sulky, Ralph delighted the fans by pacing the mile in 1:56 and 1/5th. This was not only a new Canadian record, but it tied the long-standing world record for a three-year-old on a five-eighth's mile track; Ralph had equalled the speed of Romeo Hanover at Chicago's Sportsmen's Park, back in 1955.

Ralph went on to win the West. "At Winnipeg, we were given the red carpet treatment. I was a little nervous after so much publicity that we wouldn't reach their expectations," Dr. Davis continues. There was no need to worry. Ralph set a new record for the thirteen-sixteenths-mile track and came in a ridiculous thirty lengths ahead of his nearest rival. He went on to Edmonton to take the twenty-thousand-dollar Western Canada Pacing Derby and was then recognized by the Ontario Jockey Club as "Horse of the Year."

Ralph in his first full season won $132,000, much to the delight of Elgin who had no regrets at having sold him for just $4,750. The winnings were even more remarkable because Armbro Nadir was ineligible for the major races, since the stakes payments had lapsed when he was sick. Davis says, "If I'd traded places with Glen Brown, I would likely have done the same thing; those stakes payments can certainly add up. Anyway, I'm glad for Whitey, and we get pleasure in watching Ralph whether he wins, comes second or loses."

And that's what the races are like. You win some and you lose some and hindsight doesn't do you much good.

Keystone Way, a full brother of the great sire Bye Bye Byrd, entered the Armbro stable following Elgin's $76,000 bid at Lexington, Kentucky. Keystone Way won just nine hundred dollars at the races and was sold off at a heavy discount. Tarport Rhythm had been bought from Del Miller for $2,500 and didn't look worth even that at the races. Her first filly, Armbro Irma, was sold for $3,500. Subsequently it transpired that Tarport Rhythm was an excellent brood mare and her filly was bought back for $35,000 after she won a stakes race in two minutes.

Every Armbro crop of colts had its good ones. There was Armbro Dazzle, followed by Eagle Armbro and then that standout, Armbro Flight. The year that the names began with the letter G, Governor Armbro won $365,000; Granite took the United Harness Horsemen's Stakes in Montreal; and Gazelle won $108,000. Harvey led his year in 1:59 2/5; Harold won $115,000, and Armbro Hurricane earned a reputation which was to take him to stud in Australia.

It was a good year for the letter I. Joe O'Brien took Armbro Indigo to the front to set a track record for two-year-olds at London, Ontario. Indigo won twelve of her first twenty-one starts and was in the money seventeen times. Armbro Jet was the star of the next crop and his track record makes him a currently popular stud. Armbro Jodie won $183,000, and the

118

following year a slow starter, Armbro Kerry, out of that great Adios mare Dottie's Pick, went in 1:59 and 1/5th with Joe O'Brien, and her purses were $114,000; the sort of credentials which earned Armbro Kerry the accolade of the best three-year-old pacer in America in 1970.

The Ls were another vintage crop. Armbro Laddie and Armbro Len both showed they had the stamina to break the two-minute mile. Armbro Lament, as inappropriately named as Nadir, won $111,000, while Armbro Louann added $129,923 to Armstrong winnings.

Armbro Mystic was one of the good ones in his pacing class. The Ns proved to be another great year. Armbro Nordic was a winner in the BP-Supertest Stakes while Armbro Nesbit won all over the block to collect $234,492 in a single season. In the next crop, Armbro Ouzo joined Nesbit in Duncan MacDonald's small stable and promptly won over $47,000. The Os are just coming into their prime but Armbro Omaha and Armbro Oneida and the Adios Vic colt, Armbro Ollie, were not long in returning their purchase price. Armbro Ontario chose Lexington, Kentucky, to set a world record of 1:59 2/5ths for two-year-old pacing geldings.

Harry Harvey who, years earlier, had made his name with Helicopter in the Hambletonian developed an even hotter horse. This time it was Albatross, a son of Meadow Skipper, bred and raised by Del Miller. After Harvey had driven "the big bird" to such times as 1:57 as a two-year-old, Albatross was syndicated for one and a quarter million dollars, to set a new record in standardbred horse prices. Elgin, Ted and Charlie shared ten per cent of the action, without spending a nickel. The big bird won money faster than the payments became due! Albatross, by then, trained and driven by Stanley Dancer, covered the mile in just 1:54 and 4/5ths and won $558,000 as a three-year-old.

When there was a syndicate shuffle one year later, Albatross had appreciated to two and a half million dollars and the three Armstrongs got out with a hundred per cent profit on a purchase price which they never had to make! They also pocketed their share of the purses won by Albatross. As Oscar Wilde observed, only the wealthy can practise thrift.

You win some, you lose some. And sometimes the hammer blows of fate are devastating. The 1973 yearling sale was scarred because, the autumn before, somebody had left a paddock gate open as dusk was

119

falling. A horrified gravel truck driver drove into the cream of the Armbro youngsters as they wandered onto busy Highway 10. Four were killed outright and four more had to be destroyed subsequently. Dead was a Bret Hanover filly, whose full brother had sold a year earlier for fifty thousand dollars. Also wiped out were some promising offspring of Adios Vic, Bye Bye Byrd, Airliner and Ayres. As Dr. Glen Brown sadly totted up the losses, he had to include a full-blood sister of the great Albatross.

At such a time, it helps to think about one of Star's Pride's good sons, Horton Hanover.

Joe O'Brien spent a year and a half trying to get Horton Hanover to trot and look worthy of the $39,000 invested in him. "Nothing seemed to work, but Elgin urged me to keep trying to make a racehorse of him," recalls Joe. "Finally, as a last resort, we shortened up his front toes, put on a light shoe and tried him as a pacer. It turned out that he liked the pacing gait and seemed more contented and happier with himself." Contented enough to sweep to victory in the Roosevelt events, such as the National Pacing Derby and the Nassau Pace.

A magnificent individual, Horton Hanover saved his best burst of speed until his retirement race at Hollywood Park in California. He paced the mile in 1:56 and 3/5ths to bring his lifetime earnings to $473,071. He had been in the money 100 times in 113 starts. With nineteen miles in two minutes or better, his credentials are impeccable. In his two years at stud he bred 252 mares; the 1974 stud fee was $1,500. Yes, you win some and you lose some; and sometimes when you win, you win the really big ones.

Occasionally, horses (or is it people?) have an identity problem. Soky's Tiger was first across the finish line in nine consecutive races at Yonkers and Roosevelt tracks to collect purses of $53,000; but he is none other than a classmate of Armbro Nadir. Then named Armbro Nelson, he had missed the yearling sales, because of that virus. Mariners have terrible forebodings over renaming a ship; horsemen don't seem to have the same superstitions over renaming a horse. What couldn't be changed, was Tiger's (alias Nelson's) pedigree. He is out of one of those good Adios mares, Adios Debutante, who is a full sister of a world champion, Adios Butler.

Some of the credit lines occur in distant lands. Just as the breeding prowess of the ABC Holstein-Friesians earlier rippled round the world, so

120

the impact of Armbro standardbreds was felt. In Austria, it's Armbro Duke. In Italy, Governor Armbro stands at stud. In New Zealand, Armbro stallions are staking out significant claims. Armbro Hurricane, a son of that old reliable, Dottie's Pick, sired the winner of the New Zealand Oaks and also the highest-priced yearling ever sold in New Zealand. Both Eagle Armbro and Armbro Del are also adding lustre to the Armbro name on the other side of the world.

Meanwhile, back home, there is another crop of yearlings ready for the fall sales.

Chapter 18

DO I HEAR FIFTY
THOUSAND DOLLARS?

ALL that effort around the racetrack reaches a climax with the annual sale of yearlings, and it provides an excellent example of the Armstrong "luck."

It's a brilliantly sunny Saturday in late summer. Normally on a Saturday, activity tails off around the Armstrong construction headquarters and the adjacent farms. But this Saturday is different. It's open house at the farm and the preview of the yearlings which will be offered in consignment sales at Liberty Bell in Philadelphia and at the Horse Palace in Toronto. Potential buyers have already received the glossy, illustrated and intensely documented catalogues with the pedigrees of every yearling offered for sale. An entire page is taken up with a list of the major stakes events in the United States and Canada. Check the number of these stakes with the, perhaps, forty numbers at the bottom of each page of pedigrees and you know exactly which stakes your prospective yearling is eligible for.

It's a never ending cycle. You can't get good prices for your yearlings unless they have a history of successful racing on both sides of the pedigree. Unless all those stakes payments have been made, and on time, the racing career of a yearling is marred before it can begin.

Some of that vast Armbro array of road-making equipment has been used to manicure the practice track. Water wagons have been busy spraying the roads so that they will all dry off before the first of the crowd begins to trickle in. The large farm staff, augmented by summer students, has spent two action-packed months getting the carefree yearlings from the pastures to the point where they can be led by halter safely through a thronging crowd.

No detail is left to chance. Public address systems usually emit strange sounds or sulk in silence when most needed. By 10 A.M., Charlie Armstrong is satisfied that the public address system will work perfectly at 1 P.M. And there's his father, Elgin, zipping around in the golf cart admiring the clipped grass verges and colourful rose beds. This is something of a family affair and numerous grandchildren are setting out chairs by the score. Most of the visitors will simply enjoy the afternoon's showing of the yearlings for what it is: a magnificent array of some hundred colts and fillies, each individually introduced by Glen Brown and paraded at the trot for the delight of the crowd. But the yearling show is more than this; it's a full dress rehearsal at which the yearlings can learn to cope with crowds and noise and all manner of excitements which are alien to pasture fields. When they are paraded, a few days later, before the singsong auctioneers under the arc lights in sale arenas, they'll be ready.

The crowd is swelled by the people of Brampton who look forward to this once-a-year opportunity to see the most famous local farms. But many others are potential buyers who will attend the Harness Breeders Sale at Liberty Bell Park and the subsequent sale in Toronto of the Canadian Standardbred Horse Society.

John Ferguson is there because at sale time he'll be touring Russia coaching the ice hockey greats of Team Canada. On the ice, John Ferguson is the rugged in-fighter, all elbows and knees and the will to win. Off the ice he's a soft-spoken gentleman who has his own string of a dozen standardbreds and, under the byline of "Fergy's Favourites," picks the winners for readers of the *Montreal Gazette.* "Dr. Glen Brown is a very knowledgeable man and he sure has helped me a lot. You know, without the Armstrongs, harness racing would not have achieved this success in Canada and throughout the United States."

As the standardbred fillies are paraded, one by one, to the uninitiated they must look like peas in a pod. But for the pros, the finer points are obvious. There's a colt, which seems to be the very reincarnation of Bye Bye

123

Byrd, and there's a filly which could only be from a daughter of Adios. The consensus of horsemen is that this is a great crop of yearlings, all ready for the sales.

Every colt and filly glistens in the peak of good health, but that just doesn't happen. It's a result of a pasture rotation program and a planned attack on intestinal worms. It's the result of pedicare in which the hooves are carefully trimmed and it's the result of a continuing program of preventative medicine, including vaccinations. It's also the outgrowth of a carefully monitored identification system. The upper lip of each standard-bred is tattooed under the scrutiny of the Canadian Trotting Association to ensure lifetime identification. Accurate identification is the basis of any livestock improvement program.

Indifferent to the superstitions of Armbro construction, thirteen of the fillies are being retained to increase the size of the brood mare band and replace some of the aged mares. The potential buyers like the fact that every colt is offered for sale. Some of the buyers are there because they go every year. Others have been attracted by the saturation advertising in all the North American horse journals. That celebrated Armstrong luck seems to be backed up by a great deal of carefully conceived and implemented staff work. It ranges from the breeding decisions of Elgin, Joe and Glen, to the nights that Roy Gies spends in the brood mare barn foaling the mares; to timing the departure of groom Ron Christian with loads of thirteen fillies for the Philadelphia sale. There, at Liberty Bell, the crop of yearlings awaits the arrival of the buyers. A whole year's work will be judged by the auctioneer in a matter of hours.

Meanwhile, the Canadian buyers are being flown to Liberty Bell by chartered jets from Toronto and Montreal. They are the sort of mixed bag which would be hard to conceive in any other country. There is a handful of millionaires, but they don't intrude. There are some familiar faces like that of former Lieutenant-Governor of the province of Ontario, Earl Rowe, whose lifelong joy is training and racing standardbreds and who says, "In my judgment, Armbro Flight is the greatest racing three-year-old trotter of all time." Rowe is an alert seventy-eight, who epitomizes the longevity of the fans of the trotters and pacers. He's been driving horses since he was six years of age and still begins each day with several miles at the trot.

124

Other faces are not familiar to readers of the daily press. One turns out to be a lineman for the state-owned Ontario Hydro. "I have a couple of pacers in training but I could never have come down to the sale if we had not been on strike!"

But whoever you are and whatever you are, it's a lovely way to buy. On arrival everyone gets a golden card inscribed "Special Guest," which unlocks all doors. In the evenings, there's racing at Liberty Bell Park and such stellar attractions as one of the smoothest trotters in the history of the sport, Super Bowl, who takes the Colonial one-hundred-thousand-dollar race for three-year-old trotters in 2:02 without appearing to try very hard. That hefty purse is a result of the staking system. Some 760 hopefuls had originally been nominated and numerous payments had been made. But, by race time, the field had been narrowed to six horses. Of these, the winner and three contenders had all been sired by Star's Pride, the father of Armbro Flight.

While the evenings of the two-day sale are spent in watching the proven, fast horses in action, the mornings are spent in trying to pick out tomorrow's speedsters. Each yearling has its own substantial box stall. There is a steady stream of visitors and there are potential bidders for every yearling. But the headliners get most of the attention during visiting hours. Groom Bob Anderson has to be in good physical shape himself as he trots up and down showing off Armbro O'Brien.

It is precisely noon and the public address system crackles to life with a fair warning: "There is no implied warranty made by auctioneer or consignor as to the merchantability or fitness for particular purpose of any animal offered for sale in this auction. Prospective bidders are cautioned that warranties on horses are only as stated. There is no guarantee as to racing soundness."

For some of the sale habitués this is old stuff and they are not distracted from the baked Virginia ham and Scotch-on-the-rocks which are served continuously to gold-ticketed guests in the lounge. There they may watch the progress of the sale on TV monitors and may even have a better idea where the bids are coming from than those seated at ringside. In the lounge, two girls receive telephone bids from New York and California, or is it the Taj Mahal? It becomes increasingly hard to separate illusion from reality, as a king's ransom rapidly changes hands.

The Armbro yearlings are led by their grooms to the sales pavilion in an agreed sale order; the yearlings will be sold according to the alphabetical order of their dams, beginning with those starting with the letter F. The Armbro grooms surrender their charges to the white-jacketed sales employees who will be responsible for them in the ring. The yearlings have learnt their lessons well from that open house at Brampton. They look like champions as they circle the ring; a Negro attendant waits with broom and shovel to remove any evidence that a yearling has been so indelicate as to answer a call of nature during the sale.

Just three months before, the yearlings had been revelling in their carefree life on pasture. Now their hour has come and they are ready. Their coats have that glossy sheen of good health, the ears and eyes are alert. The tails cascade from endless combings and the manes are braided with the stable colours, none other than that familiar orange peel. Their conformation and grace all testify to the success of a careful program of breeding, diet, exercise, discipline and training.

Chief auctioneer Laddie Dance has all the shrewdness of an old hand who knows how to gauge the mood of a crowd. He knows when another bid can be conjured out of the air with humour, and when a harangue will achieve the desired results. Dance is a strong and stocky individual with a rugged constitution, lungs of leather and vocal chords of nylon. He is of that triddle-de-de school of auctioneering. He seems never to be in need for a pause for breath, maintaining a ceaseless chant of bids and entreaties for the two minutes or so it takes to sell a yearling. The illuminated tote boards flash the confirmed bid of $30,000 and the four frenetic ring men each claim they have $35,000; but Laddie Dance has already spied $40,000 deep in the crowd. The auctioneer's once ruddy face turns to puce and is moistened by rivulets of perspiration. He has the crowd in the palm of his hand and he intends to keep it there.

"Lot 232, Armbro Ohio, the only son of Bret Hanover in the sale. Bret Hanover, winner of nearly one million dollars and the second-fastest harness horse of all time, the winner of every major stakes and honour offered for pacers. And a half-brother of Armbro Nesbit, by Bye Bye Byrd, and a two-year-old record of 1:59 and 1/5th." Laddie Dance emphasizes his impatience with a parsimonious bid of $40,000. *Rat-tat-tat* goes the auctioneer's gavel, and from out of the crowd comes $45,000. And who should know better the value of a half-brother of Armbro Nesbit than Duncan MacDonald whose $50,000 bid buys Ohio?

Among the 1,500 people at ringside and the more than 1,000 milling outside and around the box stalls, there are many who know the solid basis for enthusiastic bidding for the Armbro horses. People like Bill Brown, general manager of Blue Chip Farms at Wallkill, New York: "The Armstrongs have shares in our two young horses, Most Happy Fella and Overcall, so I see around thirty of their mares every year. They have the best brood mare band in the business."

Without ever appearing to change his pace, Laddie Dance continues to sell the yearlings, starting and finishing each day's sale precisely on time. When it is all over, the Armbro yearlings have averaged $13,191 for a total take of the better part of a million dollars.

The chartering of those jets from Toronto and Montreal paid off in spades. As Stan Bergstein, of the United States Trotting Association, noted in *Hoofbeats*: "The Canadian gold rush continued at an unprecedented rate. Spurred undoubtedly by the most spectacularly successful year of Canadian ownership in standardbred history." Bergstein singled out for special notice such track stars as Armbro Nesbit and Horton Hanover.

The brisk bidding of harness-racing fans from Nova Scotia, Quebec and Ontario kept many of the top prospects in Canadian hands. But other Armbro yearlings went to almost every corner of the United States: to Illinois and Ohio in the north; to Texas and Florida in the south; to New York, Massachusetts, New Jersey and Pennsylvania in the east; and California in the west. As quiet finally settled after the last lot was sold, the yearlings were already being prepared for shipment to winter training. Some were flown to California, while others were loaded in vans for Florida. Still others spent the winter north of the 49th parallel, in the care of such trainers as Herve Filion in Quebec and Jack Kopas in Ontario.

As the Canadian buyers came back through customs they were asked if they had purchased anything in the United States. They only had a little tangible reminder of their successful bids in the form of a silver coaster inscribed with the name of their newly acquired yearling. Duncan Mac-Donald had little change from a hundred thousand dollars for his week-

127

end's work—and not even a coaster—mementoes which he had generously given away. His second purchase had been Armbro Ouzo out of a Star's Pride daughter by the aptly named Speedy Scot. Before the two-year-old season was over, MacDonald had more than recouped his investment in Ouzo.

The sale of the Armbro yearlings was concluded the following week at the Canadian Standardbred Horse Society sale held at the Horse Palace at Toronto's Canadian National Exhibition grounds. Auctioneer Tom Caldwell received general agreement when he said, "I have never seen such a marked improvement in the physical quality of yearlings. You see in the ring some of the best, well-grown and well-cared-for yearlings that you will find anywhere in the United States or Canada."

But the prices bid will be far short of those of Liberty Bell; primarily because the Philadelphia consignment included yearlings by the most popular United States sires and were eligible for the major stakes races. The Toronto sale had yet to get the lift which came subsequently from the Ontario government decision to encourage horse breeders in the province by establishing Ontario stakes races. For many years, industry spokesmen such as Dr. Glen Brown had urged that this sort of incentive was essential if Canadian stables were to remain in business. Now, a small percentage of the money wagered at the tracks is used to finance the sort of purses which will encourage breeders in Ontario, just as they have for years in such neighbouring states as Ohio.

Auctioneer Tom Caldwell gasps in strained disbelief, "And you'll let me sell a filly like this for that kind of money?" His voice drips with pathos. And then he angrily castigates the crowd for its alleged apathy: "You are just cheating yourselves!"

"Yeah!" screams a ring man who has spied a bid from a huddle in the crowd. The auctioneer recognizes that in the ebb and flow of bidding a new partnership has formed. "They're having the darndest time in the board of directors," he comments and then launches into a patter to keep the sale alive while the new partnership can contemplate the strength of its resources.

"They want him so bad they can taste him," declares Caldwell, who alternates between the spiel of the practised auctioneer and exchanging banter with the ring men. Then, without apparently eyeing that newly created partnership, he senses that a decision has been reached. He extracts their higher bid with a gratitude that is fleeting. He has scented an even higher bid elsewhere. Did another money-spinner like Armbro Flight or Armbro Nesbit change hands tonight? They are hard-headed bidders out there; they have examined the conformation of each yearling and tried to appraise the true worth of the data in the pedigree. They know that they can hope and plan but that the outcome will be decided at the two- and the three-year-old races.

Probably the sale has no greater realist than ring man Paul Martin who travels with auctioneer Tom Caldwell. Martin has made a mini-career of placing those trotters and pacers which just can't beat 2:20. You won't hear fifty thousand dollars bid for them, but there is a steady market nonetheless.

Time stood still a long time ago in parts of Pennsylvania and Ontario for the stricter Mennonites and Amish; they now provide the residual market for the slowest of the jugheads. For some of these stricter religious sects, progress peaked in the seventeenth century. They prefer a buggy to a Buick and eschew most of the trappings of modern life. The pink-cheeked girls in their staid black dresses and the bearded young men in shovel hats and coveralls have a tranquility which others might envy. It's a relatively peaceful world for the standardbreds harnessed to the buggies. No more transcontinental air travel for them; not for them the garlands of flowers and photographs in the winner's circle.

Fortunately, for those standardbreds who were never within a country mile of a two-minute mile, the final indignity is shielded from their gaze. At the back of each buggy hangs a familiar two-toned triangle—the slow-moving-vehicle emblem!

Chapter 19

BOOM

THERE was nothing slow moving about the Armstrong construction enterprises during those hectic postwar years. Canada was then like a sleeping giant waking from the depression and the war years. The demand for every form of construction meant an unprecedented boom which continues after thirty years.

Arterial roads have been the key to unlocking the wealth of Canada's natural resources. The Armstrongs set new standards in both quality and speed in building highways. Road builders even formed a "Mile-a-Day Paving Club." Having built one hundred miles of the Macdonald-Cartier Freeway, alias Highway 401, and runways at Toronto International Airport, the Armstrongs landed the biggest highways contract ever awarded. This was for the widening of Highway 27, now 427, which links 401 and the airport with downtown Toronto. The highways minister acknowledged that "It was one of the most complex construction projects ever awarded in Ontario." It involved interchanges and construction of additional lanes—while the highway remained one of the very busiest in Canada! Gone were the days when a job was estimated by Elgin driving by a site on a Sunday afternoon. Armbro President Bob Charters says, "We developed job descriptions, something which was quite foreign in the earlier days of the company. Our twelve-million-dollar contract on Highway 27 was our first one planned with the use of a computer."

130

Elgin's instinct and flair for construction had been successfully wedded to new technology. The contract was completed an unprecedented ten months ahead of schedule. Completing a job ahead of schedule had long been an Armstrong trademark. It also had practical benefits. It was a wonderful morale-booster for workers at every level of the company. It was financially sound because it meant that capital was not tied up as long. No one likes the traffic disruption which is inevitable during the widening of a major highway; the Armstrong speed was appreciated both by the public and politicians.

Bob Charters parlayed this reputation into contracts for mines and pulp and paper companies across northern Ontario. The Armstrongs were no longer known as the dirt movers of Brampton, but in a single year they still might move 2.7 million cubic yards of earth! In addition, there could be over half a million tons of rock excavated; some three million tons of gravel crushed; while their asphalt plants spewed out nearly 700,000 tons of asphalt.

Some of the changes were more subtle. Alex Marquis, one of the long-time bilingual Armbro men responsible for Armstrong penetration of Quebec, noted, "When Elgin went into the bank in the late 1940s, he'd remove his hat on entering. I happened to go back into the same bank with him in the 1950s. But this time he left his hat on, which indicated to me a new independence from the banks. But Elgin remained a tremendous salesman and an actor; the best act you could see was when you asked him for a raise!"

Everything had changed and yet nothing had changed. That twelve-million-dollar assignment to rebuild Highway 27 took place on the same site as an earlier Armstrong contract back in 1937; it was there that Ollie Somerville had argued for an hour to get a ten-cent raise to fifty cents an hour. The jobs might now be planned by computer but they still had to meet Elgin's criterion that access to a job must allow "the trucks to get in and out quickly."

Young men like Bob Lowndes, born in an era of complex technology, had moved into Armbro executive positions but they still retained that early pragmatic common sense. "We don't even bid a job unless we know who is going to be in charge." Everything changes and yet nothing changes: people remain the prime consideration.

131

Periodically horse racing is rocked by fixed races and crooked drivers. Similarly, some of the most violent political explosions in Ontario have involved combines and under-the-table graft for highway contracts. Whether it's highways or horses, it just isn't Elgin's style to cut corners.

At 1:30 P.M. on a Wednesday afternoon, tenders are opened at the Ministry of Transportation and Communications tender room at Downsview, Ontario. These are always tense moments because the contracts may involve millions of dollars and perhaps two or three years' work. Sometimes, when those sealed bids are opened, the Armbro executives blanch to find that they have missed a plum by overestimating by a few hundred dollars; sometimes, as with a recent Ottawa area contract of four million dollars, their accepted bid was a whopping $800,000 below that of the nearest competitor! Bob Lowndes says ruefully, "We misjudged the competition on that bid."

The estimates on some jobs are voluminous enough to fill the Toronto telephone book. They involve a wide range of technical complexities. Some shrewd industrial intelligence is also involved: how badly do the Armbro companies need the job and how hungry are the competitors? Compiling a tender involves intensive team work. The complexities range from knowing the source and cost of materials to estimates of economic trends, interest rates and union contracts.

Cam McNab, as deputy minister in the Ontario Ministry of Transportation and Communications, can't afford to play favourites with contractors, but he acknowledges that "the Armstrongs are the deans of road builders. We could always be sure of the quality of their work and, because of their speed, the province would save carrying charges and salaries for engineering staff."

Elgin is—well, Elgin, and so some overlap between horses and highways becomes inevitable. "The Armstrongs are very competitive; if a mistake is theirs, they live with it, and if it is ours they insist on being paid," is McNab's verdict. "I remember one error of ours involving extra gravel. So I told Elgin that if he could produce the invoices I would authorize payment."

"Well, Cam," said Elgin, "at this particular pit we had to pay the farmer another two thousand dollars. I didn't pay him in cash but one of our stallions bred four of his standardbred mares!"

132

By the mid-fifties, the Canadian Tax Foundation was boggling over the annual highway investment in Canada of some six billion dollars; a figure which was soon to be dwarfed by subsequent developments. All of which was a far cry from the turn of the century. Back in 1903, when Elgin was a youngster, the first registration of automobiles was made in Ontario; the total count was two hundred. In the postwar years, the Canadian population leapt because of massive immigration . . . and the vehicles per capita doubled. Provincial planners, who prided themselves on looking twenty years ahead, soon found themselves outstripped by events. The 1980 estimates of a population of 9 million people and 4½ million vehicles could be conservative.

As the new highways spewed across Ontario, the government distributed nice little booklets proclaiming: "It is our earnest desire to protect to the full your rights as an individual." Although the Armstrongs built one-quarter of Highway 401, Elgin's worst moment came with the very first 401 contract at Tilbury in Kent County. "When we arrived on the job," says Elgin, "there must have been two hundred angry farmers there. Within ten minutes the number had doubled. The province had not even acquired their farms." This was just the first indication of incompetence and corruption, which rocked the highways department.

Other projects were closer to home and free of controversy. The Etobicoke Creek was to be tamed, after nearly a century. The first record of the Etobicoke flowing down Brampton's Main Street was made in 1854. Three years later, the *Weekly Times* noted: "Last night such an immense fall of rain took place, that early this morning the river Etobicoke rushed down with fearful velocity, and so over-spread its banks that the greater portion of Brampton was flooded." In subsequent years there were numerous floods, some loss of life and tremendous damage to property. Finally, the Etobicoke-Mimico Conservation Authority was formed and one of its major objectives was to eliminate flooding.

"The only way to get from one side of Brampton to the other during a flood was along the railroad tracks, which were some twenty feet above Main Street," says Elgin. "You could stand on the railroad bridge over Highway Number 10 and look down Main Street. Where our first office used to be, you could see people coming along in row boats and canoes.

Because some of our equipment, such as the road graders, were quite high we used them to rescue people from the stores and apartments along Main Street."

Subsequently, Elgin and Ted were able to do something of more lasting value for the town of Brampton. They built the diversion channel whose worth was soon to be tested when Hurricane Hazel dumped over eight inches of rain in a forty-eight-hour period. Brampton had the worst deluge in a century . . . but no flood. When Premier Leslie Frost officiated at the opening ceremonies, the cast of characters included familiar names which are part of the Armbro story. There was Clarence Charters, chairing the testimonial banquet, while Jack McArthur was there for the Chamber of Commerce. And representing the Etobicoke-Mimico Conservation Authority were Holstein-breeders Doug Dunton of Toronto Township and Jack Fraser of Chinguacousy.

The record of construction during those boom years of feverish activity reads like a gazetteer of Canada. There were highway jobs at Banff and Edmonton, Alberta, Barrie, Ontario, and St. Donat in Quebec. New homes were built, factories constructed and major industrial contracts completed, such as that for Canadian International Paper at Temiskaming, Quebec. Peel Construction did some work for International Harvester to recoup a little of that multi-million-dollar annual investment in new trucks. The orange Peel Construction signs became familiar from Tobermory to Thunder Bay. Montcalm Construction cut a swath through Quebec, while ABC was involved in everything from road-building to sewers and water mains, and even a luxury home subdivision. Once again there was a nice overlap between construction and the standardbreds: ABC job number 380 involved the Mohawk racetrack at Campbellville. Nowhere was the marriage of construction and horses more obvious than in the sixty-five-acre Armbro Heights development in south Brampton, where you'll find Pacer Drive, Trotters Lane and Armbro Avenue.

Sometimes, the Armstrongs were a small part of such vast undertakings as the St. Lawrence Seaway development, when they built the relocated Highway Number 2. The seaway, with its immense hydroelectric power development, was regarded by former President Dwight Eisenhower as symbols of "the accomplishments which are possible when two nations cooperate in peaceful endeavour. I am delighted that our nation is associated with our Canadian partner in this monumental development and use of the international waters of the St. Lawrence River."

Other jobs, such as the Finch Dam on a tributary of the Humber River, were all Armstrong. This provided at one site a bird's-eye view of the complexity of construction. There's an involved ballet of men and machines. The ready-mix trucks arrive in a planned sequence and a pair of cranes lift the concrete to the forms of the spillway. Despite the relatively small construction area, there are earth movers, each worth $150,000, working in a choreography which includes bulldozers and earth packers. There are quality control men taking soil samples to evaluate soil compaction. Murphy's Law—"Anything that can go wrong will go wrong"—doesn't seem to apply. When there is a crisis, it has either been anticipated or there is some prompt remedial action. Typically, the job was finished well ahead of schedule.

As the Armstrong companies prospered, the yard at Brampton sprouted trucks and vast self-propelled earth-moving equipment by the acre. A passing competitor was so intrigued by some of the recent additions of equipment that he failed to see an approaching train and hit it broadside at the level crossing. As he staggered from his wrecked car, from out of the twilight stepped a gaunt figure in a black hat and frock coat, giving every appearance of being an undertaker. He warmly shook the driver's hand and disappeared without any introduction or explanation. The shaken contractor was left with the feeling that the Armstrong efficiency extended to having an undertaker available, should his services have been needed.

Elgin was always alert to new developments in equipment. The prospect of continuous pouring of roads and runways intrigued him. He heard of a development in slip-form paving and flew down to Chicago with Bob Charters and Bob Lowndes. They drove and drove into the Ozarks on a longer journey than had been anticipated. Bob Lowndes recalls, "Elgin looked at the job for perhaps fifteen minutes and decided to buy one of the slip-form pavers for one million dollars. To get back on schedule we went to a local airport with a grass runway and rented a plane to fly back to Brampton. The only thing available was an antiquated machine with a wooden propeller. The safe midnight landing at Malton came as a relief after a hazardous journey."

For the Armstrongs those boom years were marked by the infusion of new ideas by young men, with their enthusiasm, their slide rules and their computers. There was still the contribution of Ted, with his modifications to equipment; his indestructible construction shacks and dormitories became familiar wherever the orange signs were erected. There were also Elgin's hunches. Bob Lowndes says, "Years before the route for Highway 401 was decided, Elgin had figured that the new highway had to go between certain points. He then acquired the gravel deposits so that he was in a position to bid competitively."

Success in construction for the Armstrongs came in large measure from their location and development of the aggregate materials which came out of the earth.

136

Chapter 20

OUT OF THE EARTH

Toronto's CN Tower, built on the slip-form technique which Elgin brought to Canada, reaches skyward to become the tallest structure in the world. The Toronto-Dominion Centre sprouts one tower after another to become a significant city in its own right. One out of every seven Canadian urban housing starts is in the Toronto area.

The Four Seasons-Sheraton Hotel appears almost overnight and aspires to become one of the world's great hotels. Across Nathan Phillips Square is the internationally acclaimed Toronto City Hall. Real estate authorities say that Metropolitan Toronto is the fastest-growing urban area in the world.

The rest of Canada is not merely idly watching Toronto grow. A hungry world wants the crops of the prairies. Up go huge monolithic grain storages at Churchill, at Thunder Bay and Vancouver.

Like mushrooms, the universities spring from the ground: Brock, Western Ontario, New Brunswick, Dalhousie, Guelph and Alberta. Ever bigger high schools are needed in Prince Albert, Saskatchewan, and London, Ontario. The burgeoning demand for community colleges is seen east and west from Winnipeg's Red River Community College.

New highways lace the Canadian countryside. Those four quiet lanes of 401 used to arch north of Toronto. Now, the twelve lanes (or is it sixteen?) slice through a densely built-up area and it's the "Indy 500" all over again.

The common denominator running throughout this postwar construction is the fantastic appetite for raw materials. The most significant ingredient in all that construction is a steady stream of sand and gravel and crushed rock and a score of other products which flow from the aggregate industry. Ask your average Torontonian how much aggregate he has purchased lately and you'll likely get an uncomprehending look. Most people don't buy any aggregate. But, forgive the pun, in the aggregate it means demolishing mountains and carving cavernous pits out of the land. The per capita consumption of aggregate in Ontario is now fourteen tons annually and it is expected to rise to twenty tons by 1980. Armbro Aggregates, a division of the Armstrong companies consolidated into Armbro Materials and Construction Limited, has steadily grown with the demand. It takes two to tango and it has taken two to make this Armbro enterprise successful.

Elgin, entrepreneur and extrovert, was always the front man. Elgin got the orders but it took Ted's engineering expertise to make sure the orders were filled—and on time. "You bid 'em, I'll fill 'em" is attributed to Ted.

To most Armbro business associates Ted is the unknown Armstrong. A large shambling figure with the nickname "Teddy Bear," he is the epitome of the big, rugged construction stiff. He has a phenomenal appetite for hard work and whisky. Arthritis, aggravated by the hazards of construction, has slowed him down. You'll recognize Ted and his Lincoln Continental because it is the only one in captivity with a length of hay baler twine for yanking the door closed; arthritis has made it difficult for Ted to operate without an assist from the baler twine.

Ted is a loner. Talk to the construction superintendents and to a man they can't figure out just how Ted always seems to know exactly how each job is progressing. In contrast, no one is unaware when Elgin has been on a site.

The successful teamwork of the brothers owes a great deal to the differences in their characters. There wasn't room for a second Elgin, and a Ted was essential.

In the three years of research which went into *The Armbro Story*, Elgin was always available for an interview. He had colourful and apparently total recall of what happened yesterday or fifty years ago. I never did succeed in interviewing Ted. He was too busy or he couldn't remember. I'd set up a rendezvous for taking his picture and I'd be left standing alone there with my camera. Ted had to be captured through the people who knew him best. People like Don Roberts, now a branch manager with the worldwide suppliers of heavy construction equipment, Blackwood Hodge.

Roberts was just twenty-two and working for an equipment company that was subsequently absorbed by Blackwood Hodge, when he was received into the Armstrong orbit. In the absence of all the senior personnel from the vice-president on down, Roberts took a telephone call from a Ted Armstrong. Don Roberts says, "I was told that if we wanted to make a deal on quarry equipment I'd better get out to Brampton, fast. Ted deluged me with questions, only some of which I could answer but it didn't matter, anyway. He was in a hurry and ordered the plant. So began an association which has no parallel in my life, with the possible exception of rapport with my own father. Ted not only bought the plant that day but he insisted that I go to Georgetown to set it up. He said 'I'm going to teach you the crushing business.' He did just that."

Sometimes, Roberts stayed with Ted and Dorothy for two or three weeks at a time. He went on extensive field trips with Ted and was often admonished by Mrs. Armstrong: "Take care of him, Don. You know how easily he can get pneumonia if he doesn't look after himself." When Ted flew to a construction equipment show in Paris, France, Don Roberts went along. They then went down to Lausanne, Switzerland, to visit Ted and Dorothy's daughter Susie who was at school there. Don Roberts reminisces, "After we'd spent three days in Switzerland, Ted said, 'We've done what I wanted to do, now we'll do what you want to do!' So we boarded another plane and flew to Belfast to see my wife's relatives. Ted talked endlessly of business, horses and his family. Everyone enjoyed themselves so much that even to this day every letter from our relatives includes an inquiry about Mr. Armstrong. I remember that so well because they're the only people I can ever think of who called him Mr. Armstrong."

Don Roberts found Ted stimulating because "No matter what equipment we sold Ted, he always took it into his shop for a couple of weeks. When it emerged, he had redesigned it so that it exceeded the manu-

139

facturer's specifications for output, performance and durability. He might add two thousand dollars to the cost and twenty per cent to the output. It always seemed to make sense. I'd wonder why somebody else hadn't thought about it before. By adding more buckets and chains, lengthening there, adding here, he was able to step up the capacity of an H15 asphalt plant from 80 tons per hour to about 110 tons. I know from the reaction of our suppliers that Ted is rated as one of the most knowledgeable aggregate-crushing people in the world. He was able to modify brand-new equipment so that it was capable of delivering the precise proportions of sand and stone which exacting specifications called for. A year or two later, the manufacturers would come out with Ted's modifications incorporated in their machines as standard equipment."

The same Ted who was elusive to interview and camera-shy always had the welcome mat out for Don Roberts. "It got to the point where I would seek Ted's advice on quarry plants involving customers who had no connection with the Armstrongs. I'd visit Ted's home at night and we'd sit there by the hour freely discussing problems. Often, his ideas led to design changes which solved our problems. No matter what changes he suggested, they always led to more convenient maintenance. Ted is also a very honest person; he has earned the respect of the people who work for him."

An asphalt plant is a nice trophy for any salesman's order book. Asphalt plants come in different shapes and sizes but a half-million dollars puts you in the ball park. Ted wanted a new asphalt plant and there was Don Roberts in the Brampton office to "spec it out." It wasn't a large or elaborate office and the air gradually became blue with Ted's cigar smoke; he tends to smoke a cigar at full throttle.

"Ted told me to write up the order just as Elgin came in. There I was, trapped between the two of them, each puffing away on a cigar in that small office. Elgin declared that the plant was too small and Ted refused to budge. I sat there in a quandary: whom was I to get to sign the order? Would it be Ted or Elgin or would I have to change all the specifications? I pushed the order book halfway between them and placed my pen on top."

Aggregate equipment and asphalt plants are Ted's forte. His arguments persuaded Elgin and the plant is still in use today.

The Barber-Greene Company of Aurora, Illinois, supplies a great deal of the Armbro requirements for paving machines, rock crushers and belt conveyors. In the Armstrong brothers' book, the company founders, Harry Barber and William Greene, had impeccable credentials: they were both farm boys! Around the time that Elgin was in his teens and running the Armstrong family farm, Barber-Greene designed their first bucket loader. This was followed by numerous materials-handling innovations which took the drudgery out of some previously back-breaking chores. In the 1920s, Barber-Greene had already automated snow removal, loading coal and stacking sand. By the 1930s, Barber-Greene asphalt-paving machines were laying roads in North America. When the Smith Engineering Works was merged with Barber-Greene in 1960, the new company had formidable expertise in rock-crushing equipment.

Jack Mason, of Barber-Greene, has worked closely with Ted over the years: "Armbro is a hard-driving type of company which gets the job done quickly. If you're a truck driver, don't climb into your truck at seven in the morning; have those wheels turning at seven or someone is rapping you on the back of the head. If Ted says, 'I want you to look at some paving equipment at seven in the morning,' I know I'd better be there at 6:30 A.M.; if I am not, the equipment is heading off down the road."

Jack Mason may fly Ted down to the Barber-Greene Milwaukee plant to look at a new crusher. "Once we're aboard that aircraft on the way home I know I am going to get the full treatment," says Mason. "Ted will have it figured out just how we are going to modify our latest equipment! He bought a crusher for the construction of Highway 417 near Embrun, in eastern Ontario. The crusher capacity was rated at 5,000 tons and yet Ted put 6,500 tons through that crusher. He ran two shifts of ten hours and allowed four hours for maintenance."

Ted does not have a degree but he is an engineering genius who is long on common sense. Mason adds, "Safety is a big thing in his mind. He has seen a lot of people get their arms torn off or get killed in construction. He tries to be a rough old contractor but I know that he takes such injuries personally. His modifications include extra platforms and ladders which make the machines more accessible for safe maintenance."

A slide rule and drafting board are not Ted's bag. The intricate aggregate installation at Caledon began on a piece of plywood balanced on a couple of beautiful coffee tables in Ted's home. Some of the complex aggregate machinery began with a crude sketch by Ted as Jack Mason drove the Lincoln Continental to wherever the action might happen to be.

Jack Mason knows what Ted wants; and that's an essentially practical installation which will stand continuous abuse, with a minimum of downtime. Sometimes Jack is able to take Ted's weird sketches and make them into blueprints which Barber-Greene engineers can comprehend; but often it isn't that simple.

A brand-new crusher arrived at the Barber-Greene Don Mills location. Ted was the first man on the scene every morning. For two weeks he was a familiar sight prowling round the crusher, alternately puffing on a pipe or a cigar. He finally overtaxed the patience of a welder who exclaimed, "When he draws a chalk circle on the crusher I know where he wants a hole cut. But where do I do the welding when he takes his fingers away?"

Ted Armstrong now has the august title of Chairman of the Board and the material trappings of a millionaire. But he has never shaken off the plain, practical approach of an Ontario farm boy. One summer day, Jack Mason was sailing on Georgian Bay with his family and decided to accept an earlier invitation of Ted and Dorothy to visit them at their cottage on Thunder Beach, near Penetanguishene.

"I put ashore on the beautiful Georgian Bay beach and banged on the door of an expensive home. When a maid came to the door I said I was looking for the Armstrong cottage. She thought for a minute and then replied, 'Oh! You mean the vegetable man.' And, sure enough, there was Ted's cottage down the road and behind it a log cabin and a vegetable patch of some two or three acres. He grew about ten times the vegetables they could eat. He had become a familiar sight with his disreputable old clothes and beautiful vegetables."

The Armstrongs' quarry at Trois Pistoles in the province of Quebec illustrates how the very different talents of Ted and Elgin are, in fact, complementary.

For seven years the rock was crushed at the rate of four thousand tons a day. Jack McArthur, as the Armstrongs' banker, had a special appreciation for the continuity of income provided by the quarry. For seven years the quarry provided a steady income as the ballast was hauled out in the CN cars to be used for bedding down railroad ties.

The Canadian National Railway planners had anticipated that it would be necessary to shunt cars with locomotives during the loading. Ted designed a system of conveyors which made it possible to load two cars at once in just ninety seconds. An entire train was loaded in exactly forty-five minutes.

Elgin had spread the capital cost over an expected output of one million tons. The Armstrong brothers sold over two million tons of ballast from the quarry, after the entire plant had been fully depreciated.

But Elgin is not the sort of entrepreneur to walk away from a gold mine without picking up a few stray nuggets on the way out. He moved into a downtown Montreal hotel. Somehow the word got around that Elgin was looking for a good quarry operation in the Montreal area. The first tug on the line was a big one. Jim Franceschini knew what aggressive competitors the Armstrong brothers would be in the Montreal market. He promptly purchased the used quarry equipment for a cool quarter of a million dollars, rather than risk competition. Banker McArthur regards that capital infusion as one of the key points in the fortunes of the Armstrongs.

Ted's expertise, refined at the Trois Pistoles operation, had yet another payoff. Bethlehem Steel had located iron ore deposits near Belleville, Ontario. Then, it was farmland. Now it is the Marmora mine and it's an awfully big hole in the ground. It is as aesthetically pleasing as a moon crater. It is like a grotesque Roman amphitheatre. The surface of some 120 feet of limestone is stripped, so that the opencast mine workers can get at the ore body stretching down yet another 300 feet. Stand on the lip of the mine and your eye wanders step by step to the bottom, where oversized trucks look more like children's toys.·

The rock is crushed by the Bethlehem Steel Corporation. The iron ore goes on to the United States for smelting and a by-product of trap rock remains. Trap rock is a very hard material, with some iron content, and is ideal for surfacing highways.

It was a plum to be plucked, and twelve contractors made proposals to Bethlehem. Elgin's proposal, based on Ted's record at Trois Pistoles, was accepted. The Armstrongs got a ten-year contract with an option to renew.

143

The Armstrong brothers had to invest heavily in equipment. A spur line was built to gain access to both the Canadian National and the Canadian Pacific tracks. Then, for the next one and a half years the Ontario Department of Highways refused to buy the trap rock; the delay nearly sank the overextended Armstrong company.

Elgin is the sort of persistent lobbyist who doesn't understand the meaning of no. While the highway engineers continued to specify rock from competing quarries, Elgin set out to prove the value of Marmora trap rock. Without charging a premium, he paved the Ontario Highway Number 7 bypass around Brampton with the more expensive trap rock, in preference to the cheaper limestone. He paved the main street of Brampton with trap rock to show visiting county delegations the economy of the longer-wearing material.

The trap rock would last, but the opposition to Elgin did not. For the next ten years the Armstrongs purchased trap rock from Bethlehem on the basis of twenty cents per ton. This had to be paid for only if, and when, it was picked up at the mine and hauled to the Armstrong crusher.

Subsequently, a change in the shift systems at the mine led to a change in purchasing. The trap rock was picked up from the Bethlehem stock piles at twenty-five cents per ton. For nearly twenty years a business arrangement, mutually satisfactory to Bethlehem and the Armstrongs, has continued. Trainloads of trap rock left for Windsor, Niagara Falls, Sault Ste. Marie and Toronto. Now, you'd be hard put to find a road in southern Ontario which does not have some Marmora trap rock in its surface.

The Armstrong brothers were now ready for the big one. From a modest initial investment in the Caledon Hills they have gradually acquired or optioned some two thousand acres of land: beautiful, rolling farmland, with wooded hillsides and the sylvan banks of the Credit River.

Much of the land was acquired from Conn Smythe, who had a dormant sand and gravel operation, a money-losing herd of beef cattle and a highly successful stable of thoroughbred horses. Conn Smythe, now a venerable and dapper military-looking gentleman, had fought his way up the economic ladder. A mechanical engineer, he had parlayed some Toronto gravel holdings into the sports stadium, Maple Leaf Gardens, the home of some of ice hockey's finest. It is typical of Mr. Smythe's strict standards

144

that his first gravel pit, developed in the early 1920s, has been restored. It is now Smythe Park, on Jane Street in Toronto.

The Conn Smythe Farms were the site of one of the most successful world plowing matches of recent times. Then, I didn't know Conn Smythe or the Armstrong brothers. I also was unaware of some of the little dramas that went on around that plowing match. Additional road barriers were required to control the surge of traffic as the cars in their thousands poured onto the Smythe farm. A hurried telephone call to Brampton brought up truckloads of Armstrong Brothers Company road barriers. They were just as promptly removed on the orders of Conn Smythe. He was not about to have the Smythe farms take on the appearance of an Armstrong Brothers' construction site!

Subsequently, Conn Smythe and Elgin Armstrong found that they had a great deal in common: a love of horses; a reverence for the land; a Victorian allegiance to the monarchy; and a delight in driving a bargain.

To the consternation of Armstrong executives, Conn and Elgin sat down and discussed a multi-million-dollar deal for 1,200 acres of some of the richest gravel deposits in North America. Nothing was committed to paper. More binding was that shake of the hand. For his part, Mr. Smythe has no regrets other than "Elgin's deplorable habit of eating cigars"! For the Armstrongs, it was the best financial deal they ever made.

Since digging began in 1969, many fields of pasture and wheat have gone forever. Some thirty-five acres of those Caledon Hills are consumed every year to meet the construction needs of the Toronto area.

From day one there has been a game plan. Core samples showed that there was a remarkable continuity of strata at various locations. But there are regional variations within that two thousand acres. There are large deposits of the fine and coarse material so essential to developing specific product mixes.

The first excavation was well back from the property line in a central location. Once down to water level, Ted moved in and built a unique crushing complex. Ted's crude drawings appeared on scraps of paper and cardboard. But he knew what he wanted and he eventually got it.

The Caledon plant is a low building, in contrast to many aggregate operations which soar eighty-five or more feet into the air. The spread-out plant has the advantage of delivering some eighteen different products. There is infinite flexibility in operation. Access for operation or maintenance is simple. At the centre are the office and quality control laboratory. Stretching out are two vast wings of concrete tunnels which look like the Maginot Line, but are infinitely more practical. These tunnels house endless moving belts and various hatches provide access to stored material. Regardless of the weather, the plant can be run twelve months a year. Ingredients can be selected from a central control room to provide whatever material the market currently requires. Those five-hundred-foot tunnels with their gate valves and the superstructure, and the plant, with its complex of conveyors, crushers, washers, sieves and chutes, emphasize just how sophisticated an apparently crude operation can really be. It has the precision of seed-cleaning and the repetitive procedures of auto assembly. It is simple, safe, versatile and efficient; it attracts the pros in the business from across North America.

Plant superintendent Jim Anderson marshals his forces so that supplies come from the various locations; the pit has to be worked so that the many materials are blended, and so that the aggregate deposits can be removed efficiently. Phase one is to take the pit to water level. Phase two is to extract the additional seventy feet or so located below the water line. Such deposits are often of excellent quality and can be obtained only by a suction dredge which works like a gargantuan vacuum cleaner; it sucks up twenty per cent solids and eighty per cent water and can still deliver six hundred tons of solids per hour.

Water is essential in aggregate processing. The sand particles remain as nature made them but the proportion of fine and coarse particles is effected by floating finer particles to one end of a settling chamber.

Eighteen different products out of one pit? There are different grades of concrete sand: there's a special one for asphalt making or well points; one to suit the precise needs of concrete pipe makers; and another one for mortar sand which is used for laying blocks. The bank-run has no specifications and is used for winter sanding of roads. There is a washed three-quarter-inch stone for concrete and a dry crushed stone of similar dimensions for asphalt. There's a three-quarter round which is adequate for subsurface concrete construction. Then there is clear, crushed stone for sewer beds, and various categories of crushed stone which must meet the specifications of the federal and provincial governments for their construction projects. The residual dust is blended into the asphalt ingredients. The little pea stones, all 86,000 tons of them each year, are used to roof acres of buildings.

Sand is the number one seller and over one million tons leave the Caledon pit every year. The quality control has stimulated demand for the products. Aggregate manufacturing has a direct impact on the amount of cement which is needed to make concrete of desired specifications.

I asked Jim Anderson how he rated Ted's expertise in crushing. He replied, "Crushers are Ted's field. When he does something, it is done right. He is very meticulous. Now, if he was to design that pen and pencil desk set, it would be three times the size and no normal man would be able to lift it, but it would be there for life."

Chapter 21

THE LANDSCAPE RESTORED

Elgin and Ted Armstrong grew up in an era in which hard work, success and progress were all clearly understood virtues. But eras come and eras go and the passing of that particular one disconcerts such men of action. Their contemporary, Conn Smythe, grumbles, "We're being governed to death! Governed by people who, in the army or in business, would be below you. People around Caledon knew there was gravel here when they located. Now all they want to do is to stop the gravel pits. The Armstrongs are providing work at the pits for a hundred and fifty men every day, while the government is collecting money and giving it away to provide employment for just ten or twelve people in some venture! In business today, everybody's against you!"

It is all so hard to understand. When Elgin and Ted built their first road in Dufferin County no one questioned that this was A Good Thing. Building the wartime airports was in defence of the Commonwealth. Those Armstrong gun emplacements at St. John's, Newfoundland, and at Halifax, Nova Scotia, were clear notice to Adolf Hitler that, in the event that he mastered all Europe and defeated the Russians, Britain's oldest colony and the senior Commonwealth country would be no easy pickings!

A major federal policy in the postwar years was to unite Canada with a string of large airports of international status. When the Armstrongs built runways they were carrying out not only national policy but something of a

148

clearly understood value to any businessman or vacationer. The "People or Planes" lobby was still unborn. And who even thought of the aesthetic losses when the aggregate was extracted to begin such super-highways as 401? Relieved of traffic congestion, motorists now speed from the Michigan border to Quebec. Elgin remembers proudly, "We have crushed more rock and gravel than any other contractor in Canada."

Suddenly, words like *ecology* and *environment* began cropping up with increasing frequency. Progress in the eyes of many people in the 1970s was not synonymous with more roads, more concrete, more asphalt, deeper sewers and taller buildings. A conflict between affluence and effluence meant that the popular folk hero was no longer the rugged contractor subduing the wilderness, but the articulate ecologist. Opening a gravel deposit invited controversy; closing and rehabilitating a pit brought commendation. The Royal Botanical Gardens at Hamilton was cited as an example of just how beautifully an abandoned pit can be transformed.

It became *de rigueur* to have one's words printed on recycled paper. Books appeared which would have been absolutely unthinkable in the heyday of the Armstrong brothers, when they demolished hillsides, filled swamps, built causeways and paved the pasture fields. *Say No!* is a book of the 1970s. It is the new pioneer's guide to action to save our environment. The dust jacket asks: "Have the bulldozers arrived to fill in the salt marsh, dredge the river, slash down the oak trees, level the hills and dig the foundation for the new shopping centre? . . . Say No! This book is about people who have said just that . . . . They are the new pioneers, bent not on conquering the land but on saving it from the conquerors."

Say no to the land developer? This is alien stuff for men who have taken pride in transforming "raw land" and turning it into new cities, complete with roads, sewers and acres of paved shopping plazas. The change in attitude shows in an Ontario government guide to the rehabilitation of pits and quarries: "Man is becoming increasingly aware of the necessity of maintaining and improving the quality of his environment. It is important that the aggregate producer pay serious attention to improving his public image in the community."

And what is a contractor of conservative outlook to make of a Conservative premier of Ontario who cancels any further construction of the

149

Spadina Expressway—a major traffic artery slicing through the centre of
Toronto from the trans-provincial highway? Having rattled some people's
security with that out-of-character move, Premier Davis then earmarked
1.3 billion dollars for public transportation. Curbs were placed on capital
construction of any government-funded authority. Up popped Bill Stewart,
the Minister of Agriculture, with a call to action to halt the steady erosion
by concrete of the Niagara fruit belt. Planning and land-zoning policies,
said Mr. Stewart, were needed to stem urban sprawl.

Forbes, the United States business publication, which is somewhere
out there on the extreme right wing, examined the conflict of progress and
people: "Confrontation. What happens when environmentalism confronts
economics? Somebody gets hurt. In this instance, huge segments of the
coal industry, for which only recently hopes ran so high. The environ-
mental movement has finally claimed its first industrial victim; a major
part of the $4 billion bituminous coal industry." Suddenly, open-pit mines,
like Marmora, are no longer lauded for their economy but lambasted for
their assault on the countryside.

Is there not some ambivalence in the citizen who expects others to
sacrifice their creature comforts in the interests of the environment? I
debated this moral issue with an industrialist from Hamilton as we sat on
the shoreline of Muskoka's beautiful Lake Joseph. "The quality of this
water must be preserved," he said as he spun his stogie into the lake.

"People have got too much power," mutters Elgin. The Armstrong
advertisements of yesteryear show equipment devouring the Niagara
Escarpment. Huge Peel Construction power shovels load rock into twenty-
ton Euclid trucks. The cutline under a picture of dynamite blasting
proudly announces: "Seven thousand tons of rock were blasted." In those
halcyon days there were no quarry quarrels and no pitfalls in pits.

Pow! The politically explosive *Niagara Escarpment Study* of Professor
L. O. Gertler was published. And there are the major Armbro pits, slap on
the escarpment. The Ontario Legislature passed the Pits and Quarries
Control Act which gave aggregate producers the choice of rehabilitating
their pits or paying the province to have the work done.

Citizens' groups appeared to protest the noise, the dust, the traffic, the
erosion, the depreciation of property values, the vibration and the hazards

150

attributed to aggregate production. Then along came the Niagara Escarpment Commission with its mandate to protect the escarpment in the interests of posterity.

A man in the hot seat is Bryan Burkart, a son-in-law of Elgin, who is sales manager for Armbro Aggregate Division and president of the Aggregate Producers' Association of Ontario. "Nobody wants a gravel pit in their backyard or near a recreation area," concedes Burkart. "But, remember, it was our association, which represents eight-five per cent of the industry, that made the first requests for legislative controls. Aggregate producers must accept a greater social responsibility; but they cannot implement improvements and remain competitive unless the controls are applied to everybody in the industry.

"Forty per cent of the aggregate of the Toronto Centred Region now comes from the escarpment. If these sources are denied us and we continue to deplete other sources, then the next five years are going to be critical. We believe that with responsible rehabilitation, the escarpment can still be beautiful after the extraction of aggregate."

Burkart's immediate predecessor as president of the Aggregate Producers' Association had confirmed to the Ontario government "our support of a policy that will both preserve the distinct characteristics of the escarpment and insure a balance of interests for future use. We recognize and accept the needs of the naturalist, the angler, the camper, the hiker and all those who enjoy and appreciate the scenic beauty of many sections of the escarpment."

This is an age of acts, permits and penalties, inspectors and hearings; all a far cry from the days when Elgin could find a gravel pit on a hunch and dicker with a farmer for the gravel. Like the gravel discovered by George Cowan and Bob Charters. The buxom farm wife agreed to sell the gravel for ten cents a ton— providing George gave her hired man driving lessons in her vintage touring car. "We hoped that it wouldn't start and would remain on the threshing floor of the barn," George says. "But she'd bought a new battery, and we took off faster than the chickens roosting on the seats. Luckily for us, the car shook so much that the hired man refused a second lesson!"

Elgin's pits are always left in a neat and tidy condition. Not for him the sporadic rabbit-warren approach which has marred so many potentially valuable gravel deposits. Armstrong aggregate resources are surveyed, analyzed and utilized according to carefully conceived long-range plans.

So what is Armbro doing about rehabilitation? "We have not done as much as we would have liked," says Armbro Vice-President John Maudsley. "The Caledon operation, because of the depth of the aggregate deposits, does not lend itself to piecemeal rehabilitation. But we are operating in accordance with a land-use plan prepared back in the spring of 1970."

Already, a drive down the first concession of Caledon Township gives some indication of how this currently bleak area can be rehabilitated. The road is flanked by mown, grassy banks. The white rail fences and the many trees give one the impression of pastoral peace. Yet on either side of those earth berms the aggregate extraction goes on.

A gravel pit generates some material which is good only for fill. But nothing of this nature leaves the Caledon pit. The two thousand-acre site has some areas which are currently marshy and devoid of gravel deposits. Here, the fill is dumped, and man-made islands, two or three acres in size, are being built. Around them, there will eventually be deep, clear lakes. Fringing the lakes will be some of the most prestigious building sites in Ontario. One corner is earmarked for an estate-type residential development, while other areas are destined to become parkland or golf courses.

In both 1972 and 1973, Armbro received awards from the Aggregate Producers' Association of Ontario, in recognition of the improvements being effected in the appearance of the Caledon operation.

Some twenty thousand trees are already growing to grace the homes of the latter part of this century. Perhaps the Credit River will yet be preserved as a stream of clean, clear water. The Caledon pit makes great demands on spring water, which is discharged, via a series of settling ponds, until it eventually replenishes the Credit.

And could that be Elgin Armstrong, the archetypal contractor, gazing down the wooded banks of the Credit and commenting, "This used to be great courting ground"?

As the sun went down over the beautiful Credit Valley, we drove back to Brampton. Drove past both the rehabilitated gravel areas and the scars of

today. And on to what must be one of the most unusual construction headquarters. There's the asphalt plant, with its anti-pollution scrubbers installed long before they became mandatory. We dodge the steady stream of
construction equipment which dominates Highway Number 10 and glide
between miles of white rail fences and pasturing standardbreds. We cross
the construction parking lot, which looks more like a marshalling yard. We
narrowly avoid a vast construction float and glimpse a sulky and trotter on
the half-mile track; and there, munching bird's-foot trefoil in the centre of
the oval, is Crystal Lady, the matriarch of hackney ponies.

And could that be Elgin Armstrong, aggressive pioneer, searching the
rose beds which surround the buildings? Searching for a bouquet of roses
for my wife Jean, who is to type this story.

Chapter 22

ADD CEMENT AND STIR

THE Armbro aggregate reserves of some two hundred million tons at Caledon would look good in anybody's inventory. But aggregate is a relatively bulky item with a low per-ton value. Add cement and stir, and a whole new vista of marketing aggregate opens up.

"The bricklayers want twelve dollars an hour. They are just putting themselves out of business," chuckles Elgin who sees a bright future in many forms of pre-stressed and prefabricated concrete. John Maudsley, who is responsible for both the Materials Division and long-range planning, says, "In our Materials Division we have a very nice mix of basic materials such as gravel, sand and stone, and also ready-mix and the more sophisticated pre-stress and architectural concrete products."

Maudsley is a mixture of pragmatic man and philosopher. One of Elgin's protegés, he came to the Armstrong brothers as a labourer, with some surveying and construction experience, and was a vice-president in fourteen years. "I was made a foreman in sewer construction, primarily because I was the only one who could speak English! I graduated to superintending the big residential development at Bramalea, and then one day Elgin came in and told me that next Monday morning I'd also be in charge of a new concrete ready-mix division." John Maudsley learned the construction business by practical experience. Despite his close involvement with so many Armbro operations, he developed an unusually detached point of view.

154

He admires William C. Durant (whose automobiles were in vogue when Elgin long ago showed his seed at The Royal), the architect of General Motors, who was a self-made man, a hard-driving, decisive entrepreneur, with absolute loyalty to the organization; however, Durant also had no concept of accounting or outside auditing. He had many of the attributes and drawbacks of Elgin. Maudsley also admires the business management refinements which Alfred P. Sloan, Junior brought to General Motors. Maudsley's ideal is a blend of such management and the special qualities of loyalty and enthusiasm which Elgin, apparently effortlessly, generates in all his associates.

"Working so closely with Elgin is a rare experience. It's been fun and a privilege to work with an entirely self-made man. As a student of business, I found it fascinating that he does unconsciously and instinctively many of the things which the most sophisticated business leaders and teachers advocate.

"Elgin has that tremendous ability to arrive on a job when the work is going badly. When everything had stopped for some reason on a construction site, I'd start looking over my shoulder because I'd figure he was about to arrive on the scene. He has an uncanny ability to appear when you are most vulnerable! He gets the best out of everybody; if things really are buggered up, all he will say is, 'O.K., boys, I'm sure you're going to do it. Don't worry, you'll make it work some time.' He has that faith that everything will work out well and he has a tremendous confidence in his own ability. I have seen him thrown some real good loops but he never showed it.

"I could take 101 instances of watching Elgin operate. It's right out of the textbook and it's right on the button. He's a great snow artist. Elgin was walking out of the door one day with Don McKinnon. He put his arm on Don's shoulder and said, 'You're going on your holidays tomorrow. Be damned careful you don't get into any trouble because I have to go on my holidays as soon as you get back.' And then he added, with a completely straight face, 'Can you imagine what would happen if the both of us were away at the same time?' Don knew it was a snow job but it was done so beautifully it made him feel good. Making people who try hard feel good is part of Elgin's stock in trade."

John Maudsley felt good with the responsibilities for the ABC Ready-Mix plants. Three years later, in 1964, ABC Structural Concrete Limited was formed. The products were in the two main categories of structural components and lightweight, decorative cladding which is used for facing structures.

The supermarket wars began when Dominion Stores completed its distribution centre in Toronto; it is the largest concrete structure in Canada. ABC Structural Concrete Limited built the precast and pre-stressed concrete girders for the building, which covers ten acres. The 118-foot by 900-foot loading dock is a clear span area in which even the largest tractor trailers can be wheeled around and backed up to the docks.

Don Paton, Armbro engineer, had been steadily refining his techniques, having been involved in this new concept of construction since the first pre-stressed concrete bridge was built in North America in 1950. "The first techniques came to us in Canada from Europe, where labour is cheap and materials hard to come by. In Canada, the reverse is true. Materials are relatively plentiful, while labour is expensive. The Americans added mass production so that pre-stressed materials soon won wide acceptance on this continent." The simplicity and precision of pre-cast structural components meant that Dominion Store's distribution centre was put together at the rate of twenty thousand square feet daily.

Downtown Toronto real estate is rather more expensive than the city fringes, where a building spewing over ten acres can still be economic. The Four Seasons-Sheraton Hotel has just three and a half acres across from the Toronto City Hall. The hotel soars forty-three storeys. The exterior includes over one-quarter million square feet of ABC architectural concrete panels. The self-cleansing, acrylic coating means that the hotel will not get that grimy look which mars so many city structures.

Then ABC came up with a new type of concrete building module; Corewall is a precast, pre-stressed panel which is strong, lightweight, insulated, and both load-bearing and decorative. Add cement and stir, and you have the components of instant buildings. Using concrete columns, concrete T-girders and Corewall, ABC crews have put together a twenty-thousand-square-foot building in just forty hours. The Corewall technique allows for a wide range of finishes; a variety of stone chips can alleviate the

156

monotony often associated with precast concrete. Corewall is now made in the United States under licence from ABC.

In turn, ABC imported United States technology and became a franchise manufacturer of Span-Deck. This is a versatile building component which can be made in various widths and cut to the desired length like a piece of lumber. It can be used variously for floors, roofs, ceilings and wall panels. It is economical because its cavities reduce material and transportation costs. It has a good rating for soundproofing and fire resistance and it is just about indestructible.

The dirt movers of Brampton had come a long way from the days when they were hewers of wood and drawers of water. They now had the ability to excavate a site, pour the concrete foundations and erect an entire prefabricated, concrete structure. ABC concrete products turned up all over Ontario; from the Formosa Spring Brewery at Barrie to a Sayvette department store in Windsor. Some of the contracts involved Armbro resources in just about every area of construction expertise. Other jobs involved providing a single product which might be used for the colourful exterior of a bank or the super-strength, concrete girders which carry the main Canadian National and Canadian Pacific railroads.

The Armbro business had changed from one-hundred-per-cent reliance on construction to the point where nearly sixty per cent of the revenue was coming from the Materials Division. Because of the large and continuing commitments in the construction of such major developments as the runways for the new Montreal Mirabel Airport at Ste Scholastique, the precast concrete business was sold; the purchaser, Stanley Structures, with its other acquisitions, has become a giant in a business which requires vast capital to develop modular, prefabricated-concrete housing.

Armbro had grown like Topsy, and some consolidation, with emphasis on construction, was necessary. A frenzy of activity continued in developing new projects and even new towns. The Bramalea Consolidated Developments Limited got off the ground as a combined Canadian, British and United States investment in Canada's first experiment in a completely new city; almost all of the roads and services have been built by the Armstrongs. There were also massive residential and commercial developments under contract to S. B. McLaughlin Associates. John Maudsley

157

says of Bruce McLaughlin, "He's a latter-day Elgin with lots of faith and ego . . . and a lot of polish."

The easygoing and popular Charlie Armstrong took an interest in industry affairs such as the Aggregate Producers' Association of Ontario and he was elected president of the Ontario Road Builders' Association. He also became the company stickhandler through the maze of planning ordinances which are now associated with land development.

The decision to add cement to aggregate led the Armstrongs into concepts which weren't even on the drawing board when that postwar boom started. Throughout, there was that synergism which marks so many of the Armbro endeavours. The quality control at the Caledon pit, for instance, has meant that about twenty cents can be saved on the cement component of every cubic yard of concrete. Every year, a whole new fleet of trucks hauls away some of that two-billion-ton deposit of gravel. That means hundreds of new trucks every year; the trucks have two things in common—they are built by International Harvester and they are all painted "orange peel."

Armstrong Brothers

. . . And a chunk of trap crossed my desk today.

Gordon Campbell

The Armstrongs brought the continuous-pour, slip-form concrete technique to Canada with the building of runways for Toronto's International Airport at Malton.

Armstrong Brothers

Ted: a taciturn, mechanical genius and an ideal man at home base.

Armstrong Brothers

At Trois Pistoles on the St. Lawrence River, Ted Armstrong designed the sort of aggregate plant which was the basis of success in construction.

Acton Free Press

Quarrying is a rugged business.

Allan Lloyd Photography

When you add cement to the aggregate and stir, you can get such highly sophisticated building components as this huge pre-stressed and reinforced girder.

Armbro Jet, Flight's full brother, has added new lustre to the "Airborne" family begun with their dam Helicopter.

Greenwood   " HORTON HANOVER "   August 22,1970
Owner   "THE CANADIAN PACING DERBY"   Trainer-Driver
Armstrong Bros.Co.Ltd. Purse $49,000   Joe O'Brien
              1 mile   1.59.3

Michael Burns

Joe O'Brien turned a ho-hum trotter, Horton Hanover, into a speedy pacer. Having won the Canadian Pacing Derby at Greenwood in 1:59 and three-fifths, Joe views some of the tangible trinkets with members of the Armstrong family.

Joe and Armbro Nesbit continue their winning ways at New York's Yonkers Raceway.

R. A. Lowndes

Armstrong workers paving Highway 10, Peel County's major north-south artery.

Panda Associates Photography

A convoy of ABC ready-mix trucks hauls concrete to the St. Lawrence Avenue Bridge over Toronto's Highland Creek.

Peter Lewington

John Maudsley, some-time asphalt raker, sewer foreman and now vice-president of Corporate Planning, surveys the completed bridge.

The Armstrong affairs are ever a mixture of Holsteins, horses, aggregate and construction. Agro Acres Never Fear, rich in the blood of ABC, is now favourably proven and constitutes the current ABC herd.

A young Canadian Holstein-Friesian bull pleases this group of Spaniards; some of the largest herds of Canadian Holsteins are now in such countries as Cuba, Spain and Italy.

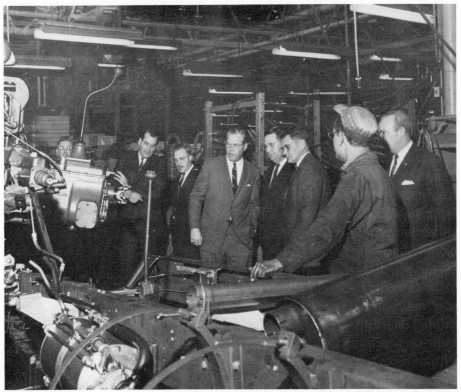

International Harvester Company

Armbro executives Bob Lowndes, Bob Charters and Don McKinnon join International Harvester Company engineers as they consider modifications for the annual Armbro truck fleet.

When Bob Charters left the Royal Canadian Air Force at the end of World War II, he started at the bottom of a still relatively small Armstrong group of companies; he now presides over a complex with 2,300 workers.

Peter Lewington

The ready-mix business was a natural evolution of aggregate production.

truck canada

September, 1973

Ontario's 1973
Truck Roadeo . . .
a lesson in
image building

Our Drivers
make the
Difference!

Inside: Trucking's role in
Intermodal Movement

Armbro transport driver Allan
Donaldson makes the cover of *Truck
Canada* magazine, after winning On-
tario's Roadeo.

Truck Canada

Happiness is winning 27 games without a loss and taking the Little NHL Championship in a third overtime period.

(Left) Open house at ABC Farms is a dry run preparing the yearlings for the annual sale. *(Right)* Potential buyers are flown in by charter jets to attend the Harness Breeders Sale at Philadelphia.

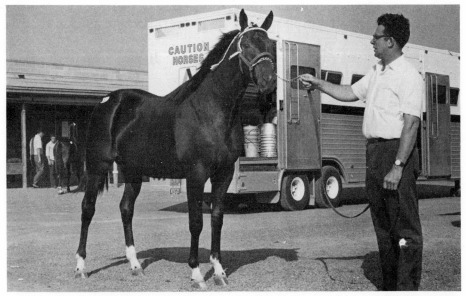

The complex of breeding, feeding, training and racing is devoted to producing a well-grown crop of yearlings ready for winter training and next summer's stakes races.

(Top) Lot Number 281, Armbro O'Brien, a Tar Heel colt out of Dottie's Pick, has reached $48,000, while auctioneer Laddie Dance looks for a new bid with an assist (right) from Stanley Bergstein of the United States Trotting Association. *(Right)* How does it feel to bring a standardbred stable to the top of the heap in North America and gross a million dollars or more at the yearling sale? If ABC Farms Manager Dr. Glen Brown's expression is any indication he's happy . . . but pooped.

Chapter 23

ORANGE PEEL

WHEN Elgin Armstrong goes shopping, he goes shopping in style. Ever since the bleak days of the Great Depression, Elgin has been buying International Harvester trucks. In recent years, his annual order has been running at around 225 trucks worth something over three million dollars.

Stuart Gardner, IHC's general supervisor of sales engineering, recalls, "All the Armstrong trucks used to be painted our standard Number 10 Green; it's a pretty unobtrusive colour. Then, the 'old man' started what he called 'orange peel.' "

This was the first time I had heard Elgin referred to as "the old man," although, as I have said, I had heard him called by many other names from "governor" to "the boss," but mostly Elgin. It was more a term of endearment than a connotation of age. Naming the paint "orange peel" was singularly appropriate because nothing is more apparent on the roads of Peel County than the distinctive orange Armbro equipment. Peel also figured in the names of such companies as Peel Express and Peel Construction, prior to all the divisions being gathered under the Armbro umbrella.

K. C. Irving, who owns an embarrassingly large part of Canada's Maritime provinces, probably has more IHC trucks on the road than anyone else. But no one, anywhere in the world, has more new IHC trucks than the Armstrongs. That single fact makes the Armbro business everybody's business, because the Armbro experience affects truck design.

The Armstrongs buy so many trucks annually, and submit most of them to such gruelling conditions, that any design weakness will show up first in their trucks. "We get quicker feedback on the Armstrong trucks than from any other source," says Gardner.

Where Lake Ontario flows out to begin the mighty St. Lawrence River, there are many extravagant summer homes which match the scenery; "summer cottage" is hardly apt for the sort of castles built by people like Randolph Hearst. The Thousand Islands was also an exciting place a few years ago, when the Armstrong brothers built the road leading to the Canada/United States International Bridge at Ivy Lea.

Every now and again there would be an orange blur, as a Peel Construction truck gathered momentum coming down the hill from the bridge. The hapless driver, sitting on the horn, was yet another indication of brake failure! Nobody kept track of the number of times the shattered road barriers were replaced but it was a minor industry all on its own.

Gardner remembers, "I was called back from vacation and engineers came from IHC in the States and from such suppliers as Wagner Electric Corporation which made the brake components. We all moved into a motel at Gananoque and started looking at those damned, broken hydraulic brake pipes; we were at our wits' end. We ran tests at our Chatham, Ontario, and Fort Wayne, Indiana, plants. Wagner began its tests. We even retained the aerospace lab at McDonald-Douglas Aircraft."

Remember Neville Shute's *No Highway*? That was the best-selling novelist's wartime story of metal fatigue which caused the loss of aircraft. Well, metal fatigue was the cause of the brake failure. All the troubleshooters finally agreed that the cause was vibration of the vacuum pipe at certain speeds. The only design change needed was the addition of an innocuous clip.

A truck is a rugged chunk of steel; loaded with upwards of twenty tons of rock, it becomes a lethal weapon should the brakes fail. Having located a weakness early in the model-year through the heavy use of Peel trucks, modifications were made on countless Chrysler and International trucks. There were no injuries or fatalities due to this particular brake

160

failure; but every truck in North America with a Wagner braking system was modified.

Dramatic design failures are rare. This is partly due to the close liaison between the Armstrongs and IHC before a new model goes into production. Some years, as many as twenty modifications are made as a result of Armstrong recommendations.

Appropriately, the key man at Armstrongs is Don McKinnon, an ex-truck driver who now heads the Equipment Division. "I was fifteen years of age and sitting on the steps of our village store on a July evening in 1943, when a big black Cadillac (it had no trim because it was wartime) passed and then backed up," recalls McKinnon. "We thought that somebody was after us and we were getting ready to run when a man, whom I later learned was Elgin Armstrong, called out, 'Would you like to come to work for me?' Because of the war, there was a shortage of men to work in the gravel pits. The next day Elgin sent the car back and I am still here working with Armstrongs!"

Too young to have a chauffeur's licence, Don McKinnon drove a truck in the gravel pits. Until he was old enough to drive on the highway, he was restricted to hauling gravel to the crushing plant. Don is yet another example of an Armstrong executive who has grown to assume a responsible managerial position without the benefit of very much formal education. But Don is long on competence and common sense.

Quite apart from the modifications which become standard on all IHC trucks, there are numerous modifications which are exclusive to the Armstrongs. These range all the way from stronger bolts to special axles, heavier spring mountings and more rugged tow-loops. Some modifications are a compromise to make the trucks more salable when they are traded in at the end of the year.

Numerous smaller companies operate entirely on used Armstrong equipment. At the end of a season you may see the prospective buyers prowling round the huge equipment lot at Brampton, jotting down the numbers of trucks which they think have best survived a tough construction season.

Still other modifications are made after sober evaluation of the economic failure rate. Gardner says, "Suppose a component has a five per

161

cent chance of failing under some particular conditions; should you build that added feature into ninety-five per cent of the trucks where it won't be needed? The engineer continually faces the economics of building the best possible truck at a competitive price which will make a profit."

An exclusive on the Armstrong trucks is a special governor line and an internal lock on the overdrive; these prevent drivers from tampering with the speed controls or exceeding the legal speed limit. Elgin long ago decided excessive highway speed is expensive; the accident rate goes up, less work is accomplished and the public is alienated unnecessarily.

Elgin's connection with International Harvester began with the purchase of his first IHC truck back in 1931. At that time, Elgin wasn't the best credit risk in the world and IHC had engineering problems. But both parties were committed to improvement. Against the odds, IHC maintained enough faith in Elgin to extend liberal credit terms—and Elgin doesn't forget that sort of cooperation.

The Armstrong truck fleet includes at least one of just about every model of truck built by IHC. These range from scout cars to pick-ups and the hybrid Travelette, which combines features of a pick-up and a sedan. There are horse vans, floats and mobile concrete mixers, and a wide range of dump trucks. This last group includes a variety of diesel and gasoline engines and various combinations of axles and transmissions designed to serve specific conditions.

Elgin annually spends millions of dollars in purchasing new IHC equipment; that sort of customer gets grade A service! Service like a special parts depot, which is maintained at the Armstrongs' Brampton headquarters.

"We go after that annual Armstrong sale just like any other business," Gardner emphasizes. "We never know if this is the year they're going to switch to Fords; you can't get the least bit complacent when you are dealing with Elgin. We are never sure if he will say he wants 175 trucks or 250. We do know that if he wants extra trucks he wants them yesterday. So we got in the habit of building an extra 25 or 30 trucks and painting them 'orange peel.' I always figured that Elgin did some lightning considerations of interest rates and took advantage of that reserve of orange peel trucks! But one thing Elgin never quibbles about is quality. If we make a case for going to the next largest size or heavier components, he always goes along with us. He doesn't like trucks smashed up and he can't stand equipment idle with breakdowns."

Truck design is no longer something which is exclusively decided by the manufacturer and modified for such unusually large customers as the Armstrongs. Truck design has become a whole new deal since Nader's Raiders and governments got involved in everything from safety to pollution abatement. And that puts engineers like Stuart Gardner in the hot seat.

"Legislation on emission control sounds fine. But everything we have done has reduced engine life and increased fuel consumption. Legislation has inevitably reduced both power and fuel economy. Theoretically, we could reduce emissions by eighty or ninety per cent but every five-per-cent improvement becomes more and more expensive. It involves more expensive metals and increases maintenance costs."

One would have to be a social outcast to argue against improved truck-braking systems. The first automobile had a man out in front with a red flag; the first four-wheel-brake vehicles had a triangular warning sign at the rear; and such signs as "Caution Air Brakes" have all been familiar during various eras of transportation.

It is technically feasible to build a braking system which will bring a gargantuan truck to a rapid stop from sixty miles per hour, without deviating from a twelve-foot traffic lane. Jump on the brake pedals in a conventional truck at that speed and a jackknife is inevitable. But equip a truck with a computer brain, which signals the braking needs to each wheel in sequence so that a locked wheel is avoided, and you have sophisticated skid control.

However, extreme sophistication can add to the risk of failure; even rocket hardware designed to reach the moon doesn't always work. "What worries me is that a driver will get in the habit of letting the computerized braking system do his thinking. He'll jump on the brakes with gay abandon. The day they don't work he'll be in the ditch and he won't know what the hell happened to him!" Gardner declares.

Now, a younger, different breed of management at Armstrongs prepares the annual truck orders. No longer is it all done on a hunch and

163

maybe—just maybe—a small calculation on the back of a packet of Marguerite cigars.

That vivid orange peel is so distinctive that any traffic violations are unlikely to go unnoticed. Don McKinnon began to get an increasing number of complaints which didn't jibe with the known location of Armstrong trucks. Now, there's a new stipulation in the annual trade-in agreement. No longer will orange peel be recycled, so to speak. Every traded-in truck will be repainted. Repainted any colour, except orange peel.

Orange peel is not a colour to be taken lightly and in vain. It became a symbol for the Armstrongs but only after a consideration of all the implications. Charlie Armstrong comments, "Orange is also the colour of the Protestant Orangemen; before we adopted it, we checked things out in the Catholic province of Quebec to see if it would be offensive on our Montcalm trucks."

Given the green light, on the orange, the Armstrongs have been busy splashing orange around Canada ever since. It is the eye-catching colour of equipment, road signs, and the various letterheads of the Armstrong companies . . . and it's also on the hard hats of the unionized work force.

Chapter 24

UNION DUES

BILL McCaugherty, the farmer who sold Elgin some of the ABC foundation stock, put his finger on the clue to the Armstrongs' success in labour relations. "I don't think that the Armstrong brothers could have built their companies to the point where they are today, without giving the fellows who worked for them a fair shake."

In the beginning, when the company was very small, there was that sense of involvement and adventure. It was a spirit which generated loyalty to the company and a determination to see it prosper.

Many of the older employees and former Armstrong workers vividly recall the wage negotiations which preceded the era of collective bargaining. When Cliff Chant, the ABC herdsman, hit Elgin for a raise, Ted interceded because "he was interested to make sure that I wasn't going to leave." Ollie Somerville's wage negotiations were typical of many. It was eyeball to eyeball; a case of one on one. "I was grading the old 27 Highway and I remember arguing with Elgin for a full hour over an increase, while the tractor sat ticking over." That man-to-man bargaining was something both parties enjoyed. Even when the companies grew bigger the personal touch remained.

For some of the younger men, construction used to be a transitory affair. To attract and keep the better-calibre workers, up went a cafeteria and a dormitory together with a recreation area, complete with billiard tables; a vast improvement for migratory workers used to hunting for a bearable boardinghouse. Long before governments became involved, the Armstrongs introduced such fringe benefits as group insurance and pension plans.

But nothing could be more alien to Elgin's style than union negotiations. His easy rapport with everyone from executives to earth movers is radically different from the trend to polarization of management and worker. Elgin demonstrated consistently throughout his business career that the welfare of employees, or associates as he usually thought of them, was inseparable from the success of the company. Nothing in his long business career could be remotely construed as being anti-employees; but entrepreneurs and unions don't usually make good bedfellows.

And then events overtook Elgin. In order to land a construction contract in Bramalea or Sudbury or operate transports in parts of Ontario, union contracts became necessities. Jack Nesbit, a private labour relations consultant, was retained and his advice proved to be valid and long lasting.

The cardinal rule in all labour relations has been to involve Armbro workers in negotiations. This contrasted with the approach of many companies and industries which surrendered negotiations to their trade association; in such an arrangement there is no involvement of the workers most intimately concerned. The direct approach of sitting around a table together eliminates some of the misunderstandings which can arise when decisions and terms are screened through various groups and individuals. Many contractors never talk to their employees about terms of contracts; entire negotiations are conducted with union representatives who have no personal contact or involvement with the company employees most concerned.

Acting on the advice of Jack Nesbit, a skilled, full-time labour relations chief was hired. Danny Fryzuk knew both sides of the negotiating table. He had twelve years' experience working for Ontario Hydro and something like eleven years as a trade union spokesman. "I saw the problems which come from empire building on either side. I learned how easy it is to get distracted and become more concerned with how things are done, rather than getting results."

The unions involved in the Armstrong enterprises have proliferated.

166

The Teamsters Union Local 230 covers many of the workers in construction, the Transportation Division, and the drivers of the ready-mix trucks. The quarry workers at Marmora are members of the United Steel Workers, while those in the structural concrete plant are members of the International Union of Allied and Technical Workers. Then there's the Labourers International Union. For the size and scope, the Armbro companies have been remarkably free of union-management conflicts. A major problem developed in the construction of Mirabel Airport, due to a feud between unions. The Quebec Federation of Labour and the Confederation of National Trade Unions fought for jurisdiction, to the detriment of Construction Montcalm, the Armbro division most active in the province of Quebec.

Maintaining a meaningful dialogue between workers and management becomes increasingly difficult when the payroll goes from hundreds to thousands. Fryzuk says, "Ask many construction workers what they do and they'll say they're carpenters or concrete foremen. Ask one of our men what they do and they are more likely to respond by saying 'I work for Armstrongs.' This bond is becoming increasingly hard to maintain now that so many construction workers see their jobs and benefits as coming from the union hiring hall and not from the company involved."

Danny Fryzuk believes that many companies sowed the seeds for the destruction of their own labour relations. "They took the easy route when they were asked to contribute a nickel or a dime in the beginning for fringe benefits. Now those benefits have swollen to, perhaps, eighty cents an hour. In a forty-hour week, that's thirty-two dollars, which the workers see as coming to them as a union benefit. We took the longer route of negotiating employer contributions to the whole host of welfare, medical and life insurance benefits."

"Do you know how much that coffee break costs me every day?" snorts Elgin. "Four thousand dollars!" But, for all that, he has learned to live amicably with the unions. When it's haymaking time, Elgin is likely to wreck farm manager Glen Brown's labour budget. "His budget never amounted to anything—the important thing is to get the hay off the fields. They [presumably all cost accountants and sundry pen-pushers] have always been bellyaching about budgets but I never listen to them—if I

167

had, I'd never be where I am today. I want top-quality hay for my horses and, as any good farmer knows, it's wise to get the hay under cover at night, so that if the weather does turn against him he can unload hay the next morning." Elgin's theory is just fine, but in practice it turns out to be rather expensive. It means using the members of the International Teamsters Union at overtime rates to haul in the bales of hay. That totes up to some thirty dollars a man for a little after-supper exercise. However, rumour has it that when there is a hint of increasing wages on the farm, Elgin will appear in the sort of raincoat Peter Falk wouldn't be seen dead in!

Credit for the good overall working relationship between the unions and management goes to Armbro President Bob Charters. This is due partly to his own experience in starting at the bottom and working up to head one of Canada's largest construction complexes. Part of his success stems from the basic philosophy of having agreements which are hammered out in the presence of the two major interested parties. Wherever companies have surrendered their autonomy and accepted blanket agreements covering an entire industry, they've made themselves vulnerable. To quote Fryzuk: "Many companies have felt that a lot of those innocuous clauses would never affect them. But those clauses become very expensive if work to rule is invoked. Strikes have now become too costly for both a company and its employees. Working to rule can sabotage a company's operations to the point where it's a total loss and the only alternative is a lockout. Meanwhile, the employees have received a full day's pay. It's a great way to run a strike. Just try to pour concrete with everybody working to rule. The devastation is terrible!"

Somehow, that rapport and willingness to work together which marked the early days of the Armstrong companies has to be fostered in an entirely different era of complex, union-management negotiations. Danny Fryzuk and Garry Smith, who heads Armbro Transport, working together with the staff seem to have found the magic formula.

Blazoned right across the back of each Transport Division truck is the slogan "Our Drivers Make the Difference!" This is no trite advertising slogan. It really means something and it really works.

"At Peel Express, we are very fortunate in having a company that's appreciative of the drivers' role," says Allan Donaldson, who was featured in an issue of *Truck Canada* devoted to the very successful Ontario Truck Roadeo. Donaldson has half a million safe driving miles and nineteen trophies which testify to his competence as the best straight truck driver in Ontario: "Trucking companies must take the right approach. Clean, well-maintained vehicles and well-trained, courteous drivers. But the whole attitude must start at the top; not enough trucking companies are placing sufficient emphasis on driver attitudes and training. When the company put that slogan on the rear end of our trucks and trailers, the company meant it and the drivers knew that they meant it."

"Managerial proficiency can be measured by the efficiency of an organization; managerial competence can also be judged by the working conditions of the labour force, the attitude of supervision towards drivers, and whether or not drivers realize that they are a vital asset to the organization," remarks Garry Smith. He counts it a failure if it ever becomes necessary to fall back on such clichés as "The management has decided" or "It is company policy" or "Due to circumstances beyond company control."

Garry Smith knows that it's just about impossible to communicate effectively with angry people. He prefers to deal with irritations before they develop into major problems. "Listening is a very important part of communications; the cause of a sullen or withdrawn attitude in a driver could be that management never listens. Gone are the days of master-servant relationships and blind obedience. Many people are asking 'Why?' The whole purpose of our driver training is to communicate our thinking to our drivers so that they understand why we want them to do the things we ask of them. We all like to be told when we have done a good job. It is just as important before the start of that job to instill confidence that you know it will be completed properly. Labour cannot function without the organization of management; management is helpless without the effort and skill of labour. Men should be made to feel part of, and an asset to, the organization for which they work. Everyone is needed by everyone else."

Gene McKinnon, like all the Armbro superintendents, knows the magic of morale. "We make all our jobs competitive. I'll pass the word along to a sewer crew or a curb crew that so-and-so did nine hundred feet today. And then they'll try to beat that record! I'll tell a shovel operator, excavating for a sewer, that one of his competitors did three hundred feet yesterday; and, sure enough, he'll go out and beat that distance!''

A Canadian who had his social security number stolen, along with various credit cards, was told that it was easier to change his name than to reprogram the computer for a new identification. In so many facets of life, the bureaucratic procedure has become more important than people. Not so at Armbro. Gene McKinnon says, ''We may have a construction safety meeting, and our workers like nothing better than to see pictures of themselves at work. In the course of a year we shoot a great deal of film on the job. It's good for a man's sense of achievement to know that he made money today. Our workers have a rough idea of what the company gets per foot for sewers or curbs; they figure out in their own heads what the job costs and they know if we are making a profit or going behind.''

Joe Nigro is a big, tough Italian-born foreman of one of the sewer crews; he flashes a wide smile from the trench and says, ''It's all right here. I've got good equipment and everything I want.'' In the tradition of the business, he brought his five-man crew with him when he started working for the Armstrongs. The manpower of Joe Nigro's sewer crew is very small in relation to the size of the Armbro companies; it also approximates the size of Armstrong Brothers' total work force in the earliest contracts back in 1929!

Elgin, in labour relations, like so many other fields, has shown himself to be far ahead of his time. When the young enthusiasts set out to build their first roads in Dufferin County, they were spurred on by Elgin's ''Tramp on her, boys!'' To a man, they knew that their efforts were needed. By 1974, Canada was a very different place and yet that same spirit still prevailed.

Chapter 25

ARMBRO ON WHEELS

"**S**OMEBODY had made an awful mistake and built the truck terminal ten times too big," says Garry Smith who is now vice-president and general manager of Armbro Transport Limited. At that time, in the late 1960s, he was involved with the forbears of Armbro Transport—Driscoll's Cartage and Storage, Peel Express, and ABC Moving and Storage. Despite the somewhat pretentious titles, the three companies combined hardly made the nucleus of a transport company.

Garry Smith was young, ambitious and eager to succeed in his new managerial position. As sales manager, he was concerned about the extensive overhead of the terminal, which was not offset by the trickle of income. He found a possible solution in the Direct Winters Company, one of the giants of Canadian trucking, which was eager to rent about half the terminal.

The terminal had been constructed on Dixie Road, just north of Highway 401. The location looked good to Direct Winters and they offered rent of two hundred dollars per door; a "door" is trucking parlance for a loading dock. The terminal had been constructed with nineteen doors on either side of a clear-span building.

Rental of four thousand dollars per month would look attractive to any sales manager whose business was in the red. "So I told Charlie Armstrong about this great opportunity and he said, 'O.K., come on up

ticated electronic equipment ranging up to some 1,400 pounds. Its major clients are Bell Canada and Xerox. Because of the high value and weight of this equipment there may be as many as six men to a single Driscoll's truck.

Driscoll's operates with a group of "D" licences. These licences name the customers such as Bell Canada, Northern Electric and Xerox of Canada. The goods of these named companies, and only these companies, may be carried anywhere in Ontario. Driscoll's is restricted in transporting other companies' goods to the confines of Metropolitan Toronto.

Peel Express operates on the simple ratio of one man to one truck. The "C" licence allows shipments to and from Toronto, Mississauga, Brampton, and Vaughan and Pickering Townships. The "A" licence allows for the delivery of goods owned by different customers. The other Peel licence is a "C". This allows for transporting full loads of a single customer's goods to or from Brampton to any other part of Ontario.

"We're just about the shortest haul 'A' carrier in the business. Our whole 'A' licence is used for pick-ups and deliveries between Brampton and Toronto," according to Garry.

Annual revenue has gone up from about ten thousand dollars the first year to a current two and a half million dollars. In every recent year, the new year's monthly business has begun with the previous year's peak. Business has grown despite a minimal increase in the number of trucks and drivers. Success is measured by the operating ratio: a ninety-per-cent operating ratio indicates that there is ten per cent for profit before taxes. Despite restrictive licensing, operating ratios with some of the larger companies exceed a hundred—which is a nice way of indicating they are going behind. The industry average is a meagre ratio of 97, while Armbro stands at 86.1. Still not good enough for Elgin. Seventy-six active years haven't slowed him down very much. Garry Smith has learned from long experience that Elgin, the consummate snow-job artist, is not himself easily conned. "Elgin will come into my office and innocently inquire if everything is in good shape. If I claim that it is, then he is likely to want to know why truck number 324 hasn't had a paint job. If I tell Elgin that we're busy, he may want to know why there are five stake trucks sitting idle in the yard. He sure keeps a fellow honest!"

174

In some men this could be an unenviable characteristic; that of hiring a watchdog and then doing the barking. "One of the keys to the Armstrongs' success has been patience. You wouldn't believe the mistakes that we made when we started," admits Garry. "We had no accounting system, no records of procedure, and everything was trial and error. We were allowed to make mistakes, simply because there was a feeling that if we succeeded everybody would profit. If things are really in a mess, Elgin won't bother you. But get a little complacent, and he won't be long in finding something to deflate you."

Treading that fine line between initiative and independent action on the one hand, and corporate policy and conformity on the other, is a difficult one for management. Elgin's long association with the International Harvester Company was explored in an earlier chapter, "Orange Peel." In view of the volume-buying muscle of Armbro, it's not a little surprising to find that Ford trucks dominate the Armbro Transport operation. To quote Garry Smith: "I'm sure that we could buy International trucks at a keener price because of the volume of business. But our maintenance people down here feel that they get better results with Ford. And the Armstrongs say, 'If that's the way you think it should be—you're running the show and that's the way it will be.' They know if they forced Internationals on us when our drivers wanted Ford, they'd end up with nothing but grief."

There are three major areas in which truck drivers can make or break a transport company. Pilferage can reach a ruinous scale; drivers can beat the system without being detected; or they can work to rule. Armbro has come close to finding solutions to all three problems.

"Pilferage is really a matter of attitude," Garry says. "If a fellow thinks of us as 'his' company then he won't do it. But we took the precaution of removing any incentive to damage cartons and goods. Who is to say that a broken carton of ketchup bottles, minor damage to skis, or some scuff marks on an expensive hi-fi set were not done accidentally? Once goods are damaged, we have to pay a claim and then dispose of the damaged goods. If a carton of food is damaged, we just send it up to the cafeteria at head office; if they can use it they pay, if they don't, they throw it out. All other damaged merchandise is sold at auction and we let our

175

drivers know when and where the sale will be held and they have to bid against the public if they want to buy." This simple expedient cuts both ways; it removes any incentive to damage goods in transit and it tends to absolve workers if damage occurs.

Beating the system in a transport company like Peel Express is very easy because the driver is out there on his own and he can do miracles for the company or he can mar its good record. To quote Garry again, "There are no two ways about it—if the drivers want to beat you, then they will, because you can't keep track of them. Our trucks are radio-dispatched but if a driver is using his cunning to beat you, you can never catch him. But suppose he uses that cunning to your advantage?" Just as Armbro policies paid off in cutting pilferage to negligible proportions, so good driver relations minimize downtime. "A driver may come to us and say, 'Why do we send two trucks into that area? I can do that work myself and we can save a truck!'"

Working to rule can cripple everything from the post office to factory assembly lines. Working to rule in the transport industry can be devastating. Some of the bigger carriers, in an effort to cope with the Teamsters Union, thought it would be a smart move to develop a master union contract. This soon proved to be an expensive, two-edged sword. When it came time to renew a contract, the union had an ideal opportunity to zero in on the worst features of each company. The master contract became complexity piled upon complexity. No responsible transport company and no conscientious dispatcher will want trucks on the highway which are not roadworthy. But supposing the speedometer fails to work? A driver operating under the massive master agreement has two options. He can drive to the nearest garage and have the speedometer repaired. But if he wants to be bloodyminded he just pulls off the highway, telephones head office, points out that under the union contract he no longer has a safe vehicle and requests that a tow truck be sent out. Armbro has avoided a great deal of grief by eschewing that master contract, which on the surface held solutions for every potential problem.

Many social and industrial relations problems stem from the same source: the machine has become more important than the human mind. At Armbro, people are still important. The emphasis on people did not come about as a result of some sanctimonious and moralistic evaluation. People came out on top because that's where the profit is. The depreciation on even a hundred pieces of transport equipment may be around one hundred thousand dollars; with each driver's wages topping ten thousand dollars per year and rising, it's obvious that wages account for many times the depreciation. Viewed in this context, the investment in people makes the outlay of even twenty-five thousand dollars in a truck shrink in significance.

It wasn't always that way. Several times during the formative years of the Armbro Transport Division, the whole thing could have gone belly-up. Even Garry Smith once left to work in the insurance business. As others had found out before him, the Armstrong companies have some things going for them which are not a customary part of modern business. Garry used that interval to learn money management. He returned to manage the Armstrong's transport business—not that the whole show then amounted to very much.

Gradually, a management team evolved. Eric Cowan, who was the first driver hired, became driver supervisor. Bert Haynes, who was the third driver on the pay roll, was promoted to sales supervisor. Driver number four, Bob Wright, is now maintenance supervisor. Among the management team of eleven, no less than nine joined the company as truck drivers.

That sort of ratio doesn't happen by chance. It all goes back to the rather involved policy of hiring drivers. All applicants for driving jobs must submit to the routine Ontario government driving test for a chauffeur's licence. "Those who pass with a minimum of ninety per cent on the written test, then become eligible for employment. Then, whenever we're looking for new drivers, we go back to this active file and call in perhaps six or seven potential drivers. They start at 7:30 in the morning and it is understood that the first two hours are on their time. When they come in, we take them down to the dock and introduce them to six or seven of our drivers. We then send them out on a routine driving assignment with one of our old hands. The newcomer doesn't handle bills or freight or anything; he is just there to drive the truck. After an hour and a half or so, they'll return and we'll interview our drivers to get their appraisal of the newcomers. You'd

177

be surprised how many of our drivers say, 'He hasn't got a very good attitude,' or maybe, 'I think the guy's looking for a job for just a few months and then he'll leave us.' This way we lose some potential drivers through a screening for attitudes. But it makes our drivers feel so much better because they are involved in the actual selection."

Those who pass the scrutiny of their peers are invited back to participate in the Armbro drivers' training course. This time, the applicants are paid from the moment they arrive. It's a six-hour show which opens with slide projectors and pictures of the management team in action. The applicants get a good idea of the sort of people they'll be working for and who is responsible for dispatching, accounting and maintenance.

The indoctrination moves along to give the potential drivers an idea of the whole sweep of the Armbro complex of companies. Pictures of the asphalt plants, highway construction, pits and quarries, tranquil brood mares and speedy two-year-olds all are flashed onto the screen.

"So they know right away what they're getting hooked into and the sort of company we are," Garry comments. Having seen the Transport Division in perspective, applicants are then put through the procedures for handling bills and some of the legal technicalities they may run into. And so it goes for that full six hours. Throughout the testing period the would-be driver is being evaluated—not just by his answers but by his attitudes. At the conclusion of that testing period the only Armbro commitment is that they will be told of the decision by telephone, that same night.

Successful applicants begin a thirty-day trial period; this is, in effect, because up to thirty days Armbro has the option of dismissing unsatisfactory drivers without getting involved in a union confrontation. Some fall by the wayside during that time of grace. The maintenance supervisor may find the new driver was hard on the truck; the dispatcher may find he can't keep a schedule or the Armbro salesman comes back with static from customers. But in most cases the feedback is quite the reverse. "We have been so pleased with the results. In the past we used to hire people if they could fog a mirror held up to their faces. That way, we went through an awful lot of grief," remarks Garry.

Hiring potentially good personnel is one thing; maintaining their enthusiasm and morale is even more difficult. Every month there is a Driver-of-the-Month award which is presented "in recognition of outstanding achievement in: good attitude, safe driving, personal appearance, low maintenance per mile and high revenue of production." The framed award is signed by both the general manager and Armbro President Bob Charters, and presented along with a pair of cufflinks. Most months, there is a meeting of drivers in the company cafeteria. There may be a speaker from the Drug Addiction Research Foundation or some other organization with some bearing on driver attitudes. Dances, baseball, hockey games and dart tournaments are all encouraged. The annual Christmas party and the worthwhile gifts for every child are the sort of things which are quite alien to companies locked in sterile management-union conflicts.

The Armbro Roadeos are always family fun affairs. Usually about thirty-five drivers will compete, cheered on by their families. The drivers compete in something akin to a barrel race. There may be pieces of radiator hose marking a course which allows one-half-inch clearance on either side of a big tandem truck. While the youngsters are rooting for dad, they also tuck into hot dogs and pop and are in turn entertained by a clown or ride ponies.

Charlie Armstrong usually awards the trophies and the overall winner moves on to compete in the Ontario Truck Roadeo. This is held at the Canadian National Exhibition in Toronto as part of Transportation Day. Thursday, August 23, 1973 was a red-letter day for Armbro driver Allan Donaldson, who won the coveted title of Grand Champion and carried home the trophy awarded by Ontario's Premier Bill Davis. Donaldson is an old hand at winning such competitions, which have the functional objective of promoting safe driving. When the National Championship was held in Vancouver, Mr. and Mrs. Donaldson were flown out to British Columbia where he came a commendable third.

Pure corn, or inspired management-labour relations? In the past couple of years there hasn't even been a single grievance. Not bad, when it is recalled a single mail carrier had managed to think up seventy grievances involving infractions of his contract!

It's an old cliché of business that you can't stand still; you either grow or you atrophy. In transportation there are two ways to grow. Additional routes can be acquired through the purchase of other companies. The likelihood of obtaining additional licences other than through acquisitions is rather slim. The other route to expansion is for Armbro to capitalize on what has turned out to be a perfect location for a transportation distribution centre. Within a stone's throw of the terminal is the fastest-growing area in Canada. But growth brings problems. Many transportation companies are becoming increasingly jaundiced with the unprofitable competition of bucking Toronto traffic for business. It makes more sense for the big carriers to concentrate on their inter-city business and off-load some of their goods so that a specialist in the business can bang on doors and run upstairs.

Garry sums up: "It makes a lot of sense to send one truck up and down a street. I anticipate that cities will encourage distribution terminals that are available to transport companies from all over Canada and the United States. I can see them coming in and saying, 'Here's our load; you deliver.' I expect to see facilities that would include refuelling and repairing transports. There are obvious advantages in having a comprehensive terminal with lodgings for drivers and such things as theatres and bowling alleys for their recreation. Everybody benefits. The big carriers continue to do what they can do best; there are new business opportunities for anyone concentrating on a distribution terminal; there would be much improved facilities for drivers; and the noise and air pollution and sheer congestion of city streets would be minimized. It could cost a quarter of a million dollars today to get a 'C' licence out of Toronto, and then you'd have to fight like hell for business. I can see that sort of money being far better spent in a terminal."

Chapter 26

SWEET AND SOUR

"**I** always went a little further than people thought I could because I had a determination to win," says Elgin. This lifelong, boundless confidence could mask an inescapable fact that life is a mixture of sweet and sour.

Elgin doesn't like to see the construction signs of his rivals erected in his own fiefdom. He regards Peel County, and especially Brampton, as pre-ferred territory; colour, Peel County orange. He is miffed to find that through overestimating by ten thousand dollars he has lost a major con-tract on Brampton's Main Street. He is consoled that the rival not only lost heavily but had to pay penalties for late completion and disruption of the town's business.

Some of the sweetest things to happen to the Armbro companies have followed association with Bruce McLaughlin's development company, S. B. McLaughlin Associates Limited, which built the huge Mississauga City Centre. This is a new city of some four thousand acres. It includes the major commercial development, Square One, with its one hundred and seventy stores, covering one and a half million square feet, making it Canada's largest shopping centre. McLaughlin is articulate and literate. A one-time high school drop-out, he returned to graduate in law and has published *100 million Canadians: a development policy for Canada*. But, like Elgin, he is an entrepreneur and one who sees land as central to all his development plans.

181

McLaughlin's Mississauga City Centre has sprung up just a stone's throw from that Derry West family farm. Also close by is Canada's other major residential, commercial and industrial development, Bramalea; as Bramalea Consolidated Developments Limited opens a new tract of land for houses, Armbro men and equipment are likely to be swarming all over the scene installing the roads and services.

Some of the sour experiences just serve to illustrate that construction is a hazardous business. A sixty-thousand-dollar crane is wrecked when it plunges over the precipice of a quarry, fortunately without loss of life. Building a causeway across the Gannon's Narrows, near Peterborough, got away to a slow start when one of the big diesel dump trucks plunged through a temporary floating bridge. Such incidents are rare but it is in the cards that they are going to occur some time. There are other hazards: such as a light-fingered thief making off with a heavy-duty bulldozer. It took a long search and a two-thousand-dollar reward to locate the missing bulldozer and return it to the Bramalea building site.

One of the sourest of sour jobs began with Elgin's supreme confidence. Tenders for a large housing development had to be submitted in the spring, when the ground was frozen and there was no chance to check on the soil structure. Elgin, the great optimist, cheerfully assumed that there would be no rock. He was mistaken. The presence of rock was just the beginning of a sequence of horrendous misfortunes. In an effort to recoup lost time, the blasters got over-zealous. The dynamite opened up not only a new sewer excavation but collapsed some five hundred feet of sewer which had already been installed.

If Elgin's optimism was typical, so was his acceptance over the sour outcome. "That's one of the breaks of the game, we learned something and now it's history." Men can do great things when much is expected of them, and yet there are no petty recriminations when they fail in an honest endeavour.

The acquisition of Wells Construction took the Armstrongs into northern and western Canada: dams, a sewage plant and a building for Atomic Energy of Canada in Manitoba, together with waterworks up at Churchill on Hudson Bay. A bridge over the St. Paul River soared 165 feet above water level; concrete for the bridge was trucked across the frozen river in minus-35-degree weather. In Saskatchewan, Wells was involved with the building of corporate offices for Husky Oil at Lloydminster, and some of the beautiful campus of the University of Saskatchewan at Saskatoon. In Alberta, much of the work was in the Edmonton area but projects extended to the Trans-Canada Highway and as far west as the Banff National Park. But Wells lacked the two ingredients which had been essential throughout the growth of all Armbro companies in eastern Canada. It didn't have the same corps of dedicated men who had been trained and promoted within the company and it didn't have the ready access to aggregate supplies.

Some aspects of construction were both sweet and sour. Elgin states: "Our most southerly work might have been building airports in the Caribbean at St. Lucia and Antigua. This was proposed under a Canadian foreign aid program which specified that the work must be done by Canadian contractors. I went down there for Wells to bid on the jobs; the government was smart to call for tenders in February. Many Canadian contractors seized the opportunity for a tax-free junket. I met three of them on the street one morning. We bid on the job but we didn't get it."

Bob Lowndes looks back on the building of the International Airport at Malton as "one of the best jobs in North America. It included our first million-dollar contract; it was also the site of a million-dollar gamble. The federal engineers were not in favour of the slip-form paving technique which would enable us to pour a runway without any joints; these could be cut later to provide for expansion. We got them to agree to our method, on condition that we remove the runway without cost if it proved to be unsatisfactory. We paved one thousand feet and they were so impressed that we kept right on going. By 1974 the federal government specified that the slip-form technique was mandatory!"

Malton Airport spread out like ripples on a pond. Some farmers felt the crunch when the federal government used powers of expropriation to acquire land for ever longer runways. Landowners on the extremity of the airport felt they were adversely affected by zoning regulations which restricted the height of any structures. Farmers claimed that their geese wouldn't set, that chickens were shaken from the roosts, while every time aircraft flew overhead cattle raced for cover. Little did the authorities,

183

planners, and contractors know that those were really halcyon days, never to return.

The second Toronto airport proposed for Pickering sparked opposition from such vociferous groups as People or Planes. Montreal's second airport will get off the ground, so to speak. But it is a development remarkably devoid of any sweetness.

When the Ste Scholastique project was first unveiled, the cost was estimated at $400,000,000 and the operational date was 1974. The first phase of development has shot up to some $540,000,000 and the airport may not be operative before 1976. Even then, the airlines are not looking forward to using it because of what they claim to be unworkable features. Various facilities will be phased in, until by 2025 six runways will be completed and an estimated fifty million passengers will use the airport.

The 1970s saw the birth of a dilemma: the demand for air travel grew, but not quite as fast as the opposition of people to new airports. Many of the world's larger international airports are now hemmed in by massive damage suits claiming property depreciation. To avoid such conflicts, nearly ninety thousand acres were acquired. With an area equal to ten per cent of the province of Prince Edward Island, it was expected that a transportation complex would evolve in harmony with industrial and commercial development. The rancour at Ste Scholastique began with the people dispossessed to make room for the airport. Mirabel is a contraction of Mirabelle, a variety of plum which grows in the area northwest of Montreal. For the three thousand landowners who surrendered nearly ninety thousand acres of land, the airport proved to be no plum. *Justice fédéral où es-tu?* typifies the anger of some farmers; they even took an effigy of Prime Minister Trudeau with them when they protested at Ottawa's Parliament Hill.

The airport proper spreads over seventeen thousand acres, considered enough to handle the ten million travellers expected annually by 1980, plus some half-million tons of air freight. Montreal is still the growth area of Quebec and accounts for forty per cent of the province's population.

When Malton was built, "progress" was applauded. Mirabel has been born in a more ecology-conscious environment. The impact of the airport has been studied by geomorphologists, plant ecologists, land-use geographers, and social psychiatrists who are concerned with the impact on people. Foresters have taken a look at the twenty-four thousand acres of forest involved and the implications for birds have been studied by wildlife biologists. A swamp may be drained and there will be a ban on the growing of such crops as corn in the buffer area, to avoid attracting birds.

Mirabel has also been the battleground of the rival Quebec Federation of Labour and the Confederation of National Trade Unions. This, despite the fact that most workers were delighted to have such a huge, continuing construction project close to Montreal. Many of Quebec's major developments in recent years have been in such places as James Bay, plagued by union violence, and northeastern Quebec, which has been called "The land God gave to Cain."

For Construction Montcalm Inc. that Mirabel plum had a bitter taste, despite the seventeen-million-dollar price tag. Stu Gardner of International Harvester says, "When I went down to check our equipment there, it just didn't look like an Armstrong job with a hundred trucks lined up for a lunch break." I asked Bert DeLong, the Montcalm project manager, why everyone was so uptight and he shrugged. "Because we're losing money." As with everything else in Quebec, there were political overtones. The construction continued long into the worst wet fall in history—so that there would be work until after the provincial election.

But for all the union disputes and the problems which stem from two levels of government and two native tongues, the building of the Mirabel runways across almost impossible terrain has been an engineering triumph. To build runways capable of sustaining the big jumbo jets, some two million tons of crushed rock are necessary. Spur lines are used to bring in trainloads of sand and cement. Huge wells and special hydroelectric lines serve the computer-controlled, concrete-making facilities.

The unique blend of construction problems at Mirabel makes Bob Lowndes say philosophically, "It certainly does not appear that Ste Scholastique will be one of our happy experiences."

Chalk up one mostly sour. An amusing sidelight was the $750,000 county road contract at Cornwall in eastern Ontario. The county engineer had anticipated that the work would take two to three years. The Armstrongs had the job done in seventy days; it was en route to Mirabel and convoys of equipment would detour to and from Brampton and the airport to complete the road in record time.

The huge Mirabel contract dwarfed earlier Montcalm work in Quebec. During the first highway jobs, Ted always knew how to smooth things over if the highway went through a village; the first item of business was to haul some crushed stone for the churchyard. The success of those jobs had hinged on Elgin's flair for getting people to enjoy exceeding their own limits, while Ted's forte was to squeeze added capacity from machines. Mirabel was something bigger and different. It was the sort of vast undertaking which could be handled only by a change to a more conventional corporate structure. The entrepreneurs who built the Armstrong companies began to give way to the young executives.

Chapter 27

"GOOD MORNING! ARMBRO"

"**G**OOD morning! Armbro," said the girl on the switchboard with a slight hesitation. She had to get used to the new name indicative of a new corporate image. Those speedy standardbreds had been bringing lustre to the Armbro prefix for years; now Armbro embraced all Armstrong enterprises. Full-page advertisements alerted the business world to the change. Six hats were pictured: the one worn by Joe O'Brien when Armbro Flight was in her prime; hard hats for quarry and construction workers; a warm, woolly hat for the Far North; and soft Armbro caps for the transport drivers. The point was well made: Armbro people do wear a lot of hats.

The original investment by Elgin and Ted of just two thousand dollars back on the eve of the depression had been parlayed into ABC Farms, ABC Moving and Storage, ABC Ready-Mix, Armbro Developments, Armstrong Brothers Company, Canam Construction and Enterprises, Dover Construction, Driscoll's Cartage & Movers, Falgar Enterprises & Rentals, Montcalm Construction Inc., W. C. Wells Construction and ABC Structural Concrete. The employees numbered over 2,300 and the businesses grossed close to seventy million dollars annually.

For the best part of the first forty years of operation the only officers and directors were Armstrongs. Elgin and Ted had been joined by Charlie in a privately owned empire which had become an anachronism in modern Canadian business. It was time for a change.

187

In 1968, Charlie Armstrong, who had brought the companies into the age of computers, became president . . . and presided over a board composed of the men whose expertise had contributed to the success of the Armstrong companies. Old faithfuls George Cowan and Jack McArthur became directors. Company solicitor Bill Dingwall, Q.C., also joined the board, along with the new guard of Bob Charters, Bob Lowndes and John Maudsley. Bruce Carruthers became secretary-treasurer and a director, in recognition of his financial ability. Elgin became chairman of the board, and Ted vice-chairman.

Three years later, that modest restructuring was followed by the next phase of streamlining the Armstrong business make-up. Elgin bowed out and Ted and Charlie moved up the corporate ladder, for the first time leaving the president's job open to a non-Armstrong, Bob Charters.

It was time for yet another change. George Cowan became a vice-president and continued to be responsible for the extensive Asphalt Division. The new guard were also made vice-presidents: Bob Lowndes for construction; John Maudsley for construction materials and corporate planning; and Garry Smith became vice-president and general manager of Armbro Transport Limited. That last change simplified the transport structure, which had previously included the three companies of Peel, Driscoll's and ABC.

Armbro Materials and Construction Limited became the umbrella for land development and all the materials from rock to ready-mix, and the construction and engineering interests. Armbro Holdings Limited assumed responsibilities for administration, finance and labour relations. Bruce Carruthers became the vice-president for finance.

The farming and horse interests, now recognized as strange ingredients of a construction company, were placed under the Armstrong Holding Company, leaving the rest of the enterprises as a more conventional business structure; reading a construction budget is hard enough without bedevilling the issue with semen sales from a Holstein bull and the stud fees of standardbred stallions.

The restructuring was much more than a change of hats and titles. Wells and the Structural Concrete companies were sold, and even such old familiar faces as Peel Construction began to disappear; the orange

188

Peel signs were replaced by orange Armbro, which didn't seem quite the same.

Budgets, that device of the pen-pushers so abhorred by Elgin, took effect. Charters points out: "People can be insurance poor and property poor. In the construction business you can become equipment poor. You can equip for your maximum requirements and then find the overhead kills you at other times when the equipment is parked."

Meanwhile, over at the cafeteria and dormitory, there were simultaneous changes. No longer would the dollar-and-a-quarter meals be served, which Elgin claimed "would cost you twelve dollars in a United States restaurant." Instead of such, allegedly, gourmet fare, the building was to house a corps of sedentary workers. No longer was the cigar package large enough for the calculations; now everything was planned, checked, budgeted, computerized and authorized. Some claimed that all the fun went out of the business in the process. But the rationalization had enabled an entrepreneurial, seat-of-the-pants operation to survive and prosper as a corporate entity.

While Elgin declined to involve the company in anything that didn't pay, Charlie represented the new generation which recognized obligations to the community. Under Charlie's leadership, Armbro sponsored baseball and lacrosse teams from Marmora to Orangeville and Brampton. Hockey stars, such as Bob Pulford and Barry Ashbee, got their start on Armstrong teams. Charlie inherited something of the winner's touch, as numerous teams went on to provincial and national championships. He also emulated his father as a trustee of the Ontario Jockey Club.

"It was Elgin who made the former structure work," John Maudsley says. "Elgin is still basically a farmer and a farmer accumulates things till the day he dies. In the future, some of our major developments may involve our land bank in joint ventures with other companies. That sort of thing isn't Elgin's style. If you've been to Las Vegas, you'll see Elgin as the type of guy who will only bet when he is throwing the dice. He is a gambler of the highest calibre; he wouldn't dream of betting on someone at the other end of the table who has a hell of a hot streak going. One of the most difficult things to accomplish as you move from a family to a corporate operation is to transfer the loyalty from individuals to the company." Or, as Bob Lowndes puts it, "There's just no substitute for having the owner, the boss, come out on the job and talk to the men."

On the credit side of the ledger, the Armbro structure makes it possible for all resources to be brought to bear to solve problems. Maudsley's view is: "I meet so many people who run down the company they work for. We do the same thing—but with a difference. We do that internally. Externally, we don't try to present the picture that we are perfect, but we do try to present the picture that we are a solid sort of firm with every part of it supported by every other part."

On the debit side, the change from a family operation to a less personal corporation presents problems for the older employees who made the whole thing possible. Alex Marquis, who turns in his steady profits from the Ottawa quarry, comments, "The last time I drove down to Brampton, they didn't know me. I was waved over with the comment, 'Visitors park over there'!"

The architects of one of Canada's success stories, both in material terms and in the development of people, recognized that a new era had arrived. Even Ted Armstrong had reached that seniority which enabled him to go to the movies half price. And Elgin, who had brought the companies from a precarious sixty-five-thousand-dollar debt in 1932 to widespread prosperity, could no longer buy a three-hundred-thousand-dollar shovel on a whim—because it wasn't in the budget.

Elgin had no social or political aspirations. He'd never been given to ostentation or good works. He would never enter the history books as a literary or economic genius. But he could look back on some incredible accomplishments. No one had achieved greater improvements in Canada's standardbreds, while the ABC Holsteins brought benefits right around the globe. He was not only part of the cataclysmic social change in Canada, he was one of its architects. It was time to take a last look at the Armbro empire with the man who had made it possible.

Chapter 28

TRAVELS WITH ELGIN

ELGIN Armstrong and Jack McArthur are to be my guides on a sortie through Ontario and Quebec looking at numerous divisions of the Armbro complex of companies. They are an ideal combination for generating background material. Jack is not just a former bank manager and currently an Armbro director. He has been a trusted confidant and adviser for over thirty years. Jack enjoys a card-index memory but he knows that I want to get the anecdotes in Elgin's words. Unobtrusively, he'll steer the conversation. I am confident that he will trigger many uniquely Elgin anecdotes. I recall the comments of some of Jack's lifetime associates, like Holstein-Friesian breeder Alex McKinney, who told me, "There wouldn't have been any ABC but for Jack McArthur who got them the money and the credit when times were tough." In a different vein, the recollections of Jake McCaugherty are also pertinent: "Jack was sent to branches of the Royal Bank which hadn't previously been making any money. But Jack never figured that he needed to spend more than four or five hours a day in the bank. 'What are the accountants for?' he'd ask. He'd go curling, or horse racing or out to the cattle shows and sales. He got to know the people who were expanding and were good credit risks. Soon, the business in the bank would pick up and the branch would be making money."

We leave the ABC horse palace aboard the big green Cadillac for a three-day trip of some two thousand miles. We have gone all of a hundred feet when we encounter Gracie, more formally known as Graciano Rodrigues, a postwar Portuguese immigrant, some-time construction worker, and then Elgin's chauffeur. Gracie has just reported for work in the black Cadillac which he uses to commute from his Toronto home to the Brampton office.

"Are you ready to go to Ottawa?" Elgin asks. "Sure," replies Gracie who is accustomed to these little bombshells. He hasn't come prepared with even a top coat, despite the chilly November day. Gracie transfers his complete baggage—a pair of sunglasses and an apple—to our Caddie. In an aside, Elgin assures Gracie that he can borrow his razor and that his bag contains an extra pair of pyjamas. This is all in delicious contrast with the conventional roles of the well-to-do businessman and his general factotum. We top up the capacious gas tank at the construction yard because, as Elgin says, "It's cheaper here." That thrifty ploy accomplished, Elgin and Jack reminisce about horses. While Elgin is talking horses, he is thinking business. By now, we have gone almost a mile and nearly past the Bovaird gravel pit. Elgin urges Gracie into a fast U-turn and back down the hill we plunge and begin a wild ride to the depths of the pit as if we were pursued by Halloween hobgoblins.

One hundred feet or more below the level of the road we stand at the edge of a small lake. Elgin chortles over the quality of the gravel which is being dredged; it is free of dirt and a premium quality. It was this same pit which had caused Elgin some disquiet shortly after we returned from Florida where, a year earlier, I had enjoyed lengthy interviews with him, without the distractions of other interests or business.

James Bovaird had opened the pit away back in 1902, having purchased the farm for just $2,800. In more recent years, the Armstrongs have paid a queen's ransom in royalties as they removed the gravel and explored the deposits to ever greater depths. To Elgin's chagrin, massive water pumps had been installed, thereby alerting the owner to the fact that yet another aggregate stratum lay below the water level. Elgin said, "I kind of scolded them on my return for starting the pumps so soon. I wanted to wait another year before I made a move to buy the property. I didn't want anybody to know what was below the water. I know, but even our own boys didn't realize. Starting those pumps could cost me thirty thousand dollars."

But Elgin is not one to dwell upon such trifles for very long. He runs an experienced eye over the stockpiles of gravel which have been denuded by the year's brisk business. "And I thought we had enough piled there for two years!" he says happily.

We pass through some once prosperous farmland, now blighted by the hand of land speculators. Elgin is also a land speculator, but not of that breed. The Armstrongs have some three thousand acres of Peel County land. Their dead elm trees, struck down by Dutch elm disease, have all been removed and burned. Fields have been cleared of stones and the old fence rows made into cropland. Excellent crops of hay and pasture are grown for the horses. Fields of oats and hundreds of acres of wheat are grown as a cash crop and for the bright straw for bedding the standard-breds. "I love farming," Elgin announces with conviction. "I like to see good crops grow . . . I'd be a farmer yet, if there had been more money in it."

But Elgin kids himself. He's too impatient to have remained a farmer. We are already behind the schedule which he has evidently set for the day. "You can open her up now," he tells Gracie. The speedometer doesn't even quiver. "Me no lose points," declares Gracie, as we adhere to the strict speed limit.

We pass the office of Peel Express which will shortly become the hub of Armbro Transportation. Elgin muses that the Transport Division turns in a steady profit. "I know what we need there is a warehouse 650 feet long. It would pay for itself in five years." That would be in time for Elgin's eighty-first birthday. He always looks ahead with the calm assurance that he will see even the longest-range plans become reality. Elgin is not ever likely to consider that he is too old to plant a tree because he personally may not enjoy its shade and beauty. Insatiable curiosity about people, places, things sparks his many interests. An aggressive, competitive urge drives him even though there are no longer material needs. He makes age irrelevant. I recall the comment of one of his engineers: "Elgin has a sense of immortality. If he doesn't live for two hundred years, then what he has built will last that long."

As we turn onto Highway 401 and head eastward we pass a truck loaded with precast concrete pipe. "Now that's a business we should be in," says Elgin. "It has a high dollar volume and a small amount of material input. Labour costs too much to pour materials on the job. We should have been in the casting of sewer pipes ten years ago."

Gracie's driving technique is to swoosh up to the car ahead, like one of those intrepid World War I fighter pilots ready to conclude a dog fight with a *coup de grâce*; just as a rear-end collision seems inevitable, Gracie swerves into the fast lane and we pass an apparently parked car. I lean forward to catch Elgin's latest homily and get a face full of Marguerite cigar smoke; I return, choking, to my tape recorder and notebook.

Clickety-click. Elgin's mind never seems to stop working. The monologues range from projected business opportunities to memories of past problems and successes. Construction is intertwined with horse racing. Elgin deplores the fact that there is an improvident expansion of harness racing. Too many cheap horses are sold which should have been slaughtered. But, characteristically, almost in the same breath, he mentions that some of his own raggle-taggle horses have been consigned to a forthcoming Toronto sale. Abruptly, he realizes that I am not just a biographer but possibly a potential horse buyer. He launches, enthusiastically, into a eulogy of a filly with a stiff leg; she could be the steal of the year and, significantly, Elgin figures she'll be in my price range.

But not all of the mature mares which are disposed of are over the hill. With a larger-than-usual choice of fillies, ABC Farms is able to dispose of some of the eighteen- to twenty-year-old brood mares. Jack says, "One of the greatest compliments that could be paid the ABC breeding program is for Hanover Shoe Farms to buy some of those aged Armbro mares."

You win some, you lose some. Elgin abruptly begins to brood over the state of affairs at Mirabel Airport under construction at Ste Scholastique. "It would be a good thing if Stanfield [the leader of the federal Progressive Conservative party in opposition in Ottawa and then a mere seat or two from being the prime minister of Canada] shut down Ste Scholastique and paid us our claims. Unstable soil that won't pack and then the wet weather—that's what killed any hope of profit from building those runways this year. It's bad now . . . but it will come out all right in the long run."

We purr along at a steady ninety miles an hour over a stretch of highway built by Peel Construction. Elgin exclaims with righteous indignation,

"And to think that our work was criticized by the Ontario Department of Highways inspector! So George Cowan went out and drove the inspector over the same stretch of highway in one of our company cars. And, hey, the bumpy road which he had criticized was smooth again. The trouble had been, not in the road, but in his own car tires. They were some of those postwar synthetic tires which wouldn't keep their shape."

We flash past a prefabricated home being hauled on a lengthy tractor trailer. "You know why they're being built?" Elgin asks rhetorically. "They're cheaper! No way can you set up on the job site and do it as cheaply as you can with precast. Times are changing so fast that if you're not ahead you'll be behind." The thought of Elgin being behind the times is too ludicrous to contemplate.

One of his most consistent traits is that of loyalty. Bonds of friendship, once forged, endure forever. He recalls J. B. Stirling, president of the E. G. M. Cape Company, contractors and structural engineers. "You know, he later became Rector of Queen's University. He is one of the best-regarded men in Canada. If you did a good job for him, he was a hundred per cent for you. He drove a hard bargain but he lived up to everything. He is one of the best men I ever did business with. He got me the International Paper Company business." Stirling was also instrumental in the formative years of the Armstrong companies. As a major federal government contractor, he was able to steer some wartime contracts in Elgin's direction.

Jack McArthur has only recently returned from a world tour during which he seized the opportunity to see some of the Armbro standardbreds which have been exported. Armstrong stallions are at stud on three continents and the continuing North American successes of the Armbro stable add to their popularity. However, Elgin is not complacent. "We've got to cull harder and improve our brood mare band, even if it is hard to get the public to pay a premium for better horses." The thought of better horses reminds him of the ones that got away. "If I ever quit in the bidding for a horse, I always found out later that I should have gone ahead and topped the bidding."

Perhaps it is a glimpse of Lake Ontario which launches Elgin into an entirely unrelated topic. He has heard of the profusion of sturgeon and whitefish in James Bay. "A man can haul in seven tons of fish in a day."

195

There's some lightning figuring at fifty cents to a dollar a pound. "Why, that puts them in a price range with beef cattle. It's just like catching beef cattle and selling them down into New York!" Apparently he had sent one of his faithful construction superintendents Cookie (Godfrey Cook of Orillia) to check out the feasibility. A refrigeration plant would be needed and arrangements for air express to New York would have to be made.

"So I am going up to Moosonee next summer to look the situation over," Elgin says. "To look the situation over" is one of his favourite phrases. But his whole outlook is revealing. He sees the fish in terms of profit. Others might have considered the contribution to employment opportunities for native peoples and an improved economic base. Such thoughts had obviously never occurred to Elgin.

There is a momentary pause in the anecdotes and I eye Elgin's shabby raincoat. Alex McCombe, manager of International Harvester Construction Equipment Sales, had earlier told me that the company annually flew Elgin down to the Hambletonian. That was in the days when companies had Lear jets as a matter of course. McCombe went on, "After the Hambletonian, we got back to the airport and Elgin realized he had left his coat at the hotel. Dr. Glen Brown and I drove twenty miles back to the hotel. The manager had the coat ready for us and I noticed that it was so shabby I wouldn't cover my dog with it! It was a beat-up old coat, frayed at the cuffs and the collar. It probably cost ten times its value to go back and fetch it!"

Elgin is slumped in the front seat resting his eyes, which are suffering the friction of contact lenses, after his double cataract operations. Suddenly he is alert and I feel the ears are more erect. We are passing over some highway under construction by a competitor. "Now that isn't the best job in the world," observes Elgin. "It is kind of sad to see how the rain has cut into it." Elgin had learned long ago not to leave any more than is absolutely necessary of an incompleted road vulnerable to the elements. Here was a good example of a grading job desperately eroded and no sign of the asphalt crews.

We pass through a swampy area and I innocently ask Elgin if this would present any problems for highway construction. "No, that would be no trick, not if you know what you are doing and have good dirt." Throughout his business life, Elgin has always known what he was

196

doing—even when he was frightening the daylights out of his colleagues and creditors. And when he speaks of "good dirt" it is with a reverence which others might use when referring to their Impressionist paintings or Georgian silver.

We leave the highway and head through the bush until we suddenly come to the spur line used by the Armstrongs to ship the trap rock out of the Marmora mine. Jack chuckles as he reminds Elgin of the different attitudes of the Canadian National Railway officials. At Trois Pistoles, Elgin had been the supplicant seeking favours. At Marmora, it was Elgin who bestowed favours on the railway. "It sure felt good to have a vice-president rush to take your hat and coat," beams Elgin.

And so to the awesome ugliness of the open-cast iron ore mine at Marmora. Now 105-ton trucks crawl up the hairpin bends as they bring the rock to the crusher. The ore body was first discovered with the use of a magnetometer in an aircraft; an ore body so large it will be worked until 1977.

We pause for refreshment at a roadside diner. Food, it appears, is a barely tolerated intrusion upon time which can be better spent. We're soon back on the highway. Elgin snaps, "This country is only good for blueberries and groundhogs." This corner of Ontario, so summarily dismissed, is one beloved by tourists and rock hounds. The tranquility of its summer lakes and the profusion of the fall colours don't rate top billing with Elgin; this shallow land doesn't grow good alfalfa or wheat.

Even Noah would have been hard put to cope with the rain which has been steadily falling all the summer over eastern Ontario and Quebec. The deeply rutted fields and the mired farm equipment, the stunted corn which could be neither sprayed with herbicides nor harvested, testify to the desperate plight of farming in the worst growing season in memory.

It's twilight as we arrive at the Ottawa quarry, to be greeted by Manager Alex Marquis. He welcomes Elgin with all the uninhibited delight of a child who has discovered Christmas. "Hi, Boss! You're looking good," Alex exclaims and promptly phones his wife to say that he won't be home for dinner. The arrival of Elgin is to be savoured in an evening of reminiscences. But first things first. The output of the quarry is totalled, as it is at the close of every working day. Nearly a million tons will leave the quarry this year. Despite our proximity to the heart of the nation's capital, the luxury of the Château Laurier Hotel is not for us. We double up at a roadside motel which doesn't even have a telephone. Elgin's taste in accommodation and food hasn't changed much since the day when sparse frugality was essential for survival. At the nearby diner, he orders with customary restraint and casts a jaundiced look at Gracie's opportunism in ordering a sirloin steak.

Long before dawn we are back on the road and heading for Embrun where the Armstrongs are building a new four-lane highway linking Ottawa with Montreal. We are greeted by Al Brannon who has that blend of rugged self-reliance and quiet confidence which is the mark of so many of the company's superintendents. Nothing, but nothing, must hold up construction. We learn that the Embrun bank has just been held up by four men who have fled with ten thousand dollars and the police in close pursuit. The bank robbers, rating freedom above sudden affluence, have cast their loot to the winds as they flee across ditches of the construction site. Al declares with outrage, "And do you know what the police asked us to do? They asked us to stop work and put down a dam to catch that floating money. No way! We were laying pipe."

These superintendents are a race apart. We move on to Willard Corrigan who has never worked for anyone but Elgin. Willard is in charge of building the reinforced-concrete bridges which will span the new highway. But the work is not proceeding fast enough to suit Corrigan, who is fearful that an early frost will delay construction and add to the costs because of the heating required during the curing process. He exhorts Elgin to go into the ready-mix concrete business in the Ottawa area because "We'd put the opposition out of business."

We drive through some of the poorly drained areas of eastern Ontario. Elgin is at a loss for words to understand how people are willing to farm under such conditions. His maxims of doing a job right and doing it fast wouldn't hold here. Neither objective is attainable without good drainage. Elgin breaks open yet another pack of Marguerite cigars and Gracie mutters, "If we gotta stay away another night and I'm gonna have to sleep with the boss, I'm gonna have a sign which says 'No Smoking'!"

Finally, we reach Mirabel, our easterly destination. It's been a tough year. Symbolically, we arrive at the job in steady rain which fails to clear the November fog. Even the hydroelectric power is off. It just didn't feel like an Armstrong job with so many workers standing around.

And then in bursts Dave Davey, general superintendent for all Peel and Montcalm construction at Mirabel. We race out in his radio-equipped car to explore runways A and B and the parking aprons which are under construction. We drive through a desolate area of second-cut bush and the small fields which testify to the marginal farming which preceded the coming of the airport. Dave is yet another man who left the Armstrongs only to return. He declares, "The experience on this job has been good for me, but it's been bad for the Armstrongs. I don't ever expect to encounter difficulties in the future which I haven't had to cope with on this job. When it didn't rain, we'd be inundated with tourists who wandered over the site, often destroying stakes and levels. We ruffled a lot of feathers when we dumped boulder-till onto the access roads to keep them out."

And the rain. The plight of farmers was accentuated by the sight of pitiful attempts to harvest weeds to stave off a winter's livestock-feeding problem. For hours we explore the fog-shrouded airport site. There's a quarry which is ten miles from the terminal, yet still within the airport boundaries. There's a spur line which brings in forty-car trains of sand. We race down the billiard-table-smooth 6,500 feet of completed runway B which represents just half the ultimate length. We lurch along access roads which have been carved through boulder-till, clay, sand, quicksand, solid rock and even muskeg.

We have encountered one sharp rock too many and have a blow-out. There is a crackling exchange on the radio, and out of the fog appears Gracie with the Cadillac. With Dave at the wheel, we're off again at high speed over terrain which would cause the GM engineers to blanch in horror.

The problems of operating hundreds of miles from home base, in another province where the mother tongue is French and the life styles are so different, have compounded construction problems. The terrain and the weather add to the hazards. For one of the first times in his career, Elgin has to admit that they are behind schedule.

Perhaps it is the sight of so many machines shut down for an early

winter but, abruptly, Elgin has seen enough and we head for Brampton.
Gracie tunes in to the weather report. It's not good. The rain is due to
change to snow and twelve inches or more can be expected. Elgin is heart-
ened by the news. "Now, when that airport is finished, we'll have to make
sure we get the snow-removal contract."

INDEX

202

203